The Tyndale New Testament Commentaries

General Editor: PROFESSOR R. V. G. TASKER, M.A., B.D.

THE SECOND EPISTLE OF PAUL
TO THE CORINTHIANS

THE SECOND EPISTLE OF PAUL
TO THE
CORINTHIANS

AN INTRODUCTION AND COMMENTARY

by

R. V. G. TASKER, M.A., B.D.

*Professor of New Testament Exegesis
in the University of London*

*Wm. B. Eerdmans Publishing Company
Grand Rapids, Michigan*

Library of Congress Catalog Card Number: 58-10234
ISBN 0-8028-1407-7

First Edition, April 1958
Sixth printing, October 1975

PHOTOLITHOPRINTED BY EERDMANS PRINTING COMPANY
GRAND RAPIDS, MICHIGAN, UNITED STATES OF AMERICA

GENERAL PREFACE

ALL who are interested in the teaching and study of the New Testament today cannot fail to be concerned with the lack of commentaries which avoid the extremes of being unduly technical or unhelpfully brief. It is the hope of the editor and publishers that this present series will do something towards the supply of this deficiency. Their aim is to place in the hands of students and serious readers of the New Testament, at a moderate cost, commentaries by a number of scholars who, while they are free to make their own individual contributions, are united in a common desire to promote a truly biblical theology.

The commentaries will be primarily exegetical and only secondarily homiletic, though it is hoped that both student and preacher will find them informative and suggestive. Critical questions will be fully considered in introductory sections, and also, at the author's discretion, in additional notes.

The commentaries are based on the Authorized (King James) Version, partly because this is the version which most Bible readers possess, and partly because it is easier for commentators, working on this foundation, to show why, on textual and linguistic grounds, the later versions are so often to be preferred. No one translation is regarded as infallible, and no single Greek manuscript or group of manuscripts is regarded as always right! Greek words are transliterated to help those unfamiliar with the language, and to save those who do know Greek the trouble of discovering what word is being discussed.

There are many signs today of a renewed interest in what the Bible has to say and of a more general desire to understand its meaning as fully and clearly as possible. It is the hope of all those concerned with this series that God will graciously use what they have written to further this end.

R. V. G. TASKER.

CHIEF ABBREVIATIONS

AV	English Authorized Version (King James).
RV	English Revised Version, 1881.
RSV	American Revised Standard Version, 1946.
LXX	Septuagint Version.
Vulg.	Vulgate (Latin) Version of Jerome, 382.
P.46	The Chester Beatty Papyrus of the Pauline Epistles (3rd century).
Aleph	Codex Sinaiticus (4th century).
B	Codex Vaticanus (4th century).
D	Codex Claromontanus.
Chrysostom	*Homilies on 2 Corinthians* (Oxford Library of the Fathers).
Denney	*The Second Epistle to the Corinthians*, James Denney (The Expositor's Bible, 1894).
Hodge	*Commentary on the Second Epistle to the Corinthians*, Charles Hodge (Edition Wm. B. Eerdmans, 1950).
Menzies	*The Second Epistle of the Apostle Paul to the Corinthians*, Allan Menzies (Macmillan, 1912).
M & M	*The Vocabulary of the Greek New Testament*, J. H. Moulton and G. Milligan (Hodder and Stoughton, 1949).
Plummer	*The Second Epistle of St. Paul to the Corinthians*, Alfred Plummer (International Critical Commentary; T. and T. Clark, 1915).
Rendall	*The Epistles of St. Paul to the Corinthians*, Gerald H. Rendall (Macmillan, 1909).
Strachan	*The Second Epistle of Paul to the Corinthians*, R. H. Strachan (Moffatt Commentary; Hodder and Stoughton, 1935).

CONTENTS

ACKNOWLEDGEMENT

Scripture quotations from the Revised Standard Version of the Bible (copyrighted 1946 and 1952 by the Division of Christian Education, National Council of Churches, U.S.A.) are used by permission.

AUTHOR'S PREFACE

'HAVING faithfully listened to the great teachers that you may enter into their thoughts', Ruskin wrote in *Sesame and Lilies*, 'you have got this higher advance to make; you have to enter into their hearts.' In the case of some writers the former of these duties imposed by great literature upon its readers is the more easy to discharge; with others the latter is the less difficult. In this second group the author of 2 Corinthians should be placed; for there can be few readers of this intensely personal and most moving document who remain insensitive to the quick-beating pulse of its writer, however difficult they may sometimes find it to follow his thought. So unsparingly does he unbosom himself, and so freely does he give expression to his changing moods and feelings, that the way lies open to an intimate understanding of the apostle's heart with all its tenderness, its joys and its fears.

Students of this Epistle have testified with remarkable unanimity that this has been the experience that the reading of 2 Corinthians has enabled them to enjoy. Three illustrations may suffice. Paul's intimate self-revelation found a ready response in the sensitive, pastoral heart of George Herbert. 'What an admirable Epistle', he exclaimed, 'is the second to the Corinthians! How full of affections! He joys and he is sorry, he grieves and he glories; never was there such care of a flock expressed, save in the great Shepherd of the fold, who first shed tears over Jerusalem and afterwards blood.' Very different from George Herbert was Benjamin Jowett, yet for him too the self-disclosure of the apostle expressed in magnificent paradox is the most outstanding feature of this letter. 'The Second Epistle to the Corinthians', Jowett wrote, 'is perhaps the most characteristic of the apostle's mind. . . . Glorying and humiliation; life and death; a vision of angels

9

strengthening him, the "thorn in the flesh" rebuking him; the greatest tenderness, not without sternness; sorrow above measure, consolations above measure, are some of the contradictions which were reconciled in the same man.' Finally, we may quote a similar testimony from the incisive and comprehensive essay on Paul by W. R. Inge: 'Of all the Epistles, the second to the Corinthians is the one which contains the most intimate self-revelations, and few can read it without loving as well as honouring the author.'

It is perhaps partly this comparative ease of access to the apostle's heart that makes it difficult for the reader to enter quickly into his thought, for the intensity of feeling that is seeking to find expression in the rapidly moving narrative often makes both sequence and syntax difficult. But the greatest complexities of 2 Corinthians arise from its strongly marked epistolary character. It has been well called 'the most letter-like of all the letters of Paul'. And, as Adolf Deissmann truly added, 'its great difficulty is due to the very fact that it is so truly a letter, so full of allusions and familiar references, so pervaded with irony and with a depression which struggles against itself, matters of which only the writer and the original readers understood the purpose, but which for the most part we can ascertain only approximately.'[1] As a result, translators and interpreters are faced with problems which often admit no certain solution. Not least are these difficulties felt by a commentator who bases his work on the text of the traditional English versions.

It cannot be said that these versions are at their best in their rendering of 2 Corinthians. The makers of the AV gave most memorable translations in many parts of this Epistle which do full justice to the original; but over-anxiety to be strictly literal led them to perpetrate sentences which cannot be regarded as good English and are sometimes less than intelligible. What, for example, have readers made in the past, or what can they be expected to make today, of such a sentence

[1] *Bible Studies*, p. 47.

as 'I told you before, and foretell you, as if I were present, the second time; and being absent now I write to them which heretofore have sinned, and to all other, that, if I come again, I will not spare' (xiii. 2)? The RV was a great improvement, for not only was it based on better Greek MSS, but it removed many of the archaisms and obscurities of its distinguished predecessor; but often it too failed to rise above the level of 'translation English'. The RSV, which I have often quoted in this commentary, seems to have achieved a considerable degree of success in embodying many of the more probable interpretations of modern scholars while, at the same time, retaining the general structure of the RV. It is, however, very widely recognized that the case for a generally accepted second version of the New Testament in good contemporary English is nowhere stronger than in 2 Corinthians.

R. A. Knox has recently pointed out[1] that such a translation of 2 Corinthians calls for a good deal of courage on the part of the translators. It can, however, be undertaken with confidence, because modern students of this Epistle have undoubtedly contributed much to a more intelligible reconstruction of the historical situation it presupposes. Earlier commentators almost invariably based their interpretation on the assumption that only one visit to Corinth had been paid by the apostle before he wrote this letter; that the letter alluded to in 2 Cor. ii. 3 and vii. 8 was the canonical 1 Corinthians; and that the offender of 2 Cor. ii. 5–11 was the perpetrator of incest mentioned in 1 Cor. v. It is now very generally agreed, for reasons that will become apparent in the commentary, that these three suppositions are all improbable. Many recent commentators are also convinced that the exegesis of the Epistle is rendered easier by the adoption of what is to them the highly probable hypothesis that chapters x–xiii are not the closing section of the letter to which they have become attached, but the final part of the letter referred to in 2 Cor. ii. 3. For reasons stated in the Introduction, I am unable to accept this view;

[1] *The Epistles and Gospels*, p. 215 (Burns, Oates and Washbourne).

and the present commentary is written on the assumption that the Epistle is intelligible as a unity.

In preparing this volume I have found the commentaries of Charles Hodge, Allan Menzies and James Denney of the greatest help, though in somewhat different ways. The first, recently republished by Eerdmans,[1] contains a very thorough exegesis of the Epistle from the standpoint of Reformation theology. The second is more valuable for the understanding of its historical setting, and presents the case for the integrity of the Epistle clearly and convincingly. As it has been out-of-print for a long while it is not as widely known as it deserves to be. The third is a most eloquent and moving exposition of the great themes of the document from the pen of a great scholar and evangelist, who shows their relevance for the Christian Church today.

I have of necessity been mainly concerned in the present volume with the attempt to elucidate the text, so that the reader may be able to enter more fully into the apostle's thought. I could, however, desire nothing more than that he should also be helped by what I have written to make 'the higher advance' of which Ruskin spoke. For it is clear that Paul was what he was, a new man in Christ, because of the grace of God (see 1 Cor. xv. 10). He himself was a living embodiment of the truth of the gospel he proclaimed, the gospel of the all-sufficient grace of Christ (see 2 Cor. iii. 5, ix. 8, xii. 9). In 2 Corinthians he does not methodically expound this gospel, but he alludes to it in most memorable expressions. The theological emphasis of this Epistle may truly be said to be upon the constraining love of Christ (v. 14), whose grace was shown in His becoming poor for our sakes (viii. 9) and in His being made sin that we might be made the righteousness of God in Him (v. 21). The weakness in strength, and the strength in weakness, both so wonderfully displayed in the life and death of Jesus, were in a scarcely less wonderful manner reflected in the life of His apostle, who could say,

---

[1] Wm. B. Eerdmans Co., Grand Rapids, Michigan.

'Most gladly will I glory in my infirmities, that the power of Christ may rest upon me' and whose greatest paradox is expressed in the words 'When I am weak, then am I strong' (xii. 9, 10). To enter therefore into the heart of Paul is to know Jesus and the power of His resurrection.

R. V. G. TASKER.

INTRODUCTION

THE Second Epistle to the Corinthians was almost certainly written in the late autumn of AD 56 from a town in Macedonia, after Paul had met Titus who had brought back reassuring news of the condition of the Corinthian church. The provenance of the Epistle can clearly be deduced from vii. 5, 7; and Macedonia, or more specifically Philippi, is mentioned as the place of origin in some MSS, though that information may be no more than an inference from the Epistle itself. The tone of the references to Paul's meeting with Titus in ii. 13 and vii. 6 ff. certainly lead us to suppose that that meeting had taken place very recently.

The Christian church at Corinth consisted mainly of converted Gentiles of little or no education or social standing. 'Not many wise men after the flesh', Paul says in 1 Cor. i. 26, 'not many mighty, not many noble' had been called at Corinth, and they found it extremely difficult to keep the unity of the spirit and hold high the torch of Christian morality in a decadent and corrupt society. When we remember that a Corinthian in ancient Greek drama was more often than not portrayed as a drunkard or a prostitute, and that it was from the lower strata of the population that Paul's converts were for the most part drawn, we are not surprised that the Corinthian Christians were a source of considerable anxiety to him.

The only information to be obtained from the Acts of the Apostles about Paul's visits to Corinth is that he spent some two years in the city on his first journey into Europe, and during those months the Corinthian church was founded (Acts xviii. 1–11). As Gallio became proconsul during the latter part of Paul's stay (xviii. 12), and we know from other sources that he entered upon his proconsulship in AD 51 or 52, Paul's first visit to Corinth can be dated with confidence. Some five or six years later the apostle spent three months in Greece, presumably at Corinth, before retracing his steps through Macedonia on what was destined to be his last journey to Jerusalem (see Acts xx. 3). For his dealings with the Corinthians between these two visits we are entirely dependent upon what can be learned from the canonical First and Second Epistles to the Corinthians.

1 Corinthians, as we discover from xvi. 8, was written at Ephesus during the latter part of Paul's stay there, a visit which is described in some detail in Acts xix. In this Epistle we are told that the apostle had already written a letter to the Corinthians telling them 'not to company with fornicators' (v. 9). Though some scholars maintain that a fragment of this letter has survived in 2 Cor. vi. 14–vii. 1, it is more probable that it is no longer extant. It was in all probability a brief letter meant for the Corinthians alone, and not suitable, as the canonical Epistles of Paul were suitable, for wider circulation. The Corinthians may well have deliberately destroyed it. This letter is usually referred to by scholars as the 'previous' letter. Not long after it was written Paul received information from members of the house of Chloe (1 Cor. i. 11) that immorality was still rife at Corinth, that a flagrant act of incest had been committed, and that the Corinthians were splitting into factions and carrying their quarrels into the pagan law-courts. It is possible that from the same source he also learned that the 'previous' letter had not had the results that he had desired, and that in one respect it had been misunderstood (see 1 Cor. v. 9–11). It was partly to deal with this information and partly to answer some difficulties which the Corinthians themselves had referred to him in a letter, probably brought to him by Stephanas, Fortunatus and Achaicus (1 Cor. xvi. 17), that Paul wrote the canonical First Epistle. We do not know for certain who was the bearer of this letter. It is suggested in this commentary that Titus may have been sent with it with instructions to expedite the organization of the collection

which is mentioned for the first time in 1 Cor. xvi. 1 ff. 1 Corinthians would have been delivered at Corinth the best part of a year before the writing of 2 Corinthians. (See notes on viii. 6 and ix. 2.)

In the course of 1 Corinthians the apostle mentions that he has sent Timothy to Corinth, to 'bring you', he tells the Corinthians in iv. 17, 'into remembrance of my ways which be in Christ, as I teach every where in every church.' The further reference to Timothy at the end of the letter, 'If Timotheus come, see that he may be with you without fear' (xvi. 10) need not imply uncertainty in the apostle's mind as to whether Timothy would arrive at Corinth, for 'if' can equally well mean 'when' as in the RSV translation. Paul's reference does, however, suggest that he was doubtful whether his beloved child in the faith, who would seem to have been not only young but also unduly diffident, would really be able to deal with offenders at Corinth in the fearless way that the situation might demand.

The course of events between the writing of the canonical First and Second Epistles to the Corinthians is difficult to reconstruct in detail, but certain points are clear. It is a reasonable conjecture that Paul's anxiety about Timothy was justified, and that the latter returned to Ephesus with a report that there had been little or no improvement at Corinth. It would seem that Paul then hurried over to Corinth himself. He had intended, as he had stated in 1 Cor. iv. 19, to visit the Corinthians *soon*; and his words in xvi. 5 imply that this visit would be paid after he had passed through Macedonia. That plan was in all probability now abandoned, and he crossed over to Corinth as quickly as he could by the direct sea-route. Though nothing is said of this visit in Acts, its occurrence would seem to be a necessary inference from certain passages in 2 Corinthians. The words of i. 23 'To spare you I came not as yet to Corinth', and of ii. 1 'I determined that I would not come again to you in heaviness' imply a recent and a painful visit (see the commentary on both these passages); for the original visit to Corinth when the church was founded could scarcely be said to have been undertaken in sorrow. Moreover, in xii. 14 the apostle writes 'The *third* time I am ready to come to you', and in xiii. 1 'The *third* time I am coming to you', both of which passages, as is suggested in the commentary, are most naturally interpreted on the assumption that two visits had already been made. This second visit is conveniently spoken of by scholars as the 'painful' visit. When Paul returned to Ephesus at its conclusion, he apparently made up his mind that, in spite of any previous promises to the contrary, he would not visit Corinth again until the situation there had considerably improved.

It is usually assumed, and probably correctly, that it was to avoid paying a third visit to Corinth immediately that Paul now wrote a letter so severe in tone that subsequently he somewhat regretted having written it. This letter is usually known as the 'painful' letter. Many scholars are of the opinion that its closing portion survives in chapters x–xiii of 2 Corinthians, but reasons are given in the next section of this Introduction for rejecting this hypothesis. The existence of this 'painful' letter as the *third* letter addressed by Paul to the Corinthians would seem to be a necessary deduction from his words in vii. 8 'For though I made you sorry with a letter, I do not repent, though I did repent', and from his statement in ii. 4 'Out of much affliction and anguish of heart I wrote unto you with many tears'. It is most unlikely that these are references to the 'previous' letter, for on that assumption they would appear to be very belated and not obviously relevant; and, though the identification of the 'painful' letter with 1 Corinthians was almost invariably made by earlier commentators, it is seen to be increasingly improbable the more the apostle's descriptions of it are considered. For, while it may well be true that he suffered 'much affliction and anguish of heart' in writing about the perpetrator of incest in 1 Cor. v, and about the failure of the Corinthians to grasp the seriousness of his action; and while it may also be true that a list of other verses from 1 Corinthians might also be compiled, about which it could be said with some plausibility that Paul might later have regretted the tone in which he had written, nevertheless it is very difficult to suppose that the writing of 1 Corinthians *as a whole* caused him grief, and this is the real point at issue. Moreover, while it could perhaps be reasonably surmised that Paul wrote as he did in 1 Cor. v to 'know the proof of the Corinthians, whether they were obedient in all things' (see ii. 9), yet it could not be said that this was the primary reason for the writing of the *entire* letter, as the reference in ii. 9 seems to imply. The letter in question, which was written 'with many tears', would seem to have been far more limited in scope than 1 Corinthians and far more intense in character. The supposition therefore that it was a letter written subsequent both to the 'previous' letter and to the canonical First Epistle would seem to be inevitable.

What then were the contents of the 'painful' letter? We have to answer this question solely from the references to it in 2 Corinthians. It is reasonable to suppose that it dealt with some offence given to Paul in person during the 'painful' visit; for immediately after the reference to the 'painful' letter in ii. 4 Paul says, in effect, in the somewhat enigmatical words of verses 5 and 6, that if a certain person has caused grief, it is not Paul himself who has been grieved, except in part, but to some extent all the Corinthians.

For a detailed exegesis of these verses the commentary should be consulted. It may be said here that what Paul seems to be implying is that he himself was the victim of the insult, but that he refuses to consider this untoward incident as a matter relating merely to the offender and himself. In verse 9 he adds, 'To this end also did I write, that I might know the proof of you, whether ye be obedient in all things.' We may surely infer both from this and from the contents of the report subsequently brought back by Titus (vii. 9–11), that Paul had made it clear to the Corinthians in the 'painful' letter that his relations with them would remain at a standstill until they had dealt with the offender. By such punishment alone could the offence which had struck at the heart of the fellowship between the Corinthians and their apostle be in a real sense 'abolished', and all parties concerned become free to make a fresh beginning.

Nevertheless, after writing this letter Paul, as we have seen, was somewhat troubled in conscience. Had he written *too* severely? Had he expected too much from these young converts? Had he perhaps shown too little of 'the meekness and gentleness of Christ'? (see x. 1). In order to obtain reliable information at the earliest possible moment about the effects the letter might have upon the Corinthians, Paul instructed Titus, who, we may assume, was its bearer, to rejoin him as soon as possible. The apostle may well have also informed Titus that he himself would move on to Troas for further evangelistic work (see ii. 12) as soon as his work at Ephesus was over, and there await the return of his ambassador. In any case, it was most probable that, even if he went to Troas without Titus having been previously informed of his intentions, he would sooner or later meet him. The events narrated in Acts xix may have compelled Paul to leave Ephesus sooner than he had intended. If the reference in 2 Cor. i. 8, 9 is to the incident recorded in Acts, the apostle would appear to have been in far greater danger from the uproar caused by the devotees of the goddess Diana than the narrative in Acts would lead the reader to suppose. But this reference is not certain. What is certain is that Paul underwent suffering that nearly proved fatal before he eventually arrived at Troas. We can picture him in that seaport town anxiously looking out for his friend among the passengers who landed from the ships from Macedonia, and interrupting his evangelistic work for the purpose, though that work was of immediate importance. As he says in ii. 12, 'A door was opened unto me of the Lord.' But his mind was still much occupied with the state of affairs at Corinth; and the long days of waiting for Titus' return eventually became intolerable to the overstrained and always impetuous apostle. He could find, he says in vii. 5, no rest in his spirit. He was 'troubled on every side; without were fightings, within were fears'. He therefore decided to cross over to Macedonia alone, hoping that he would meet Titus somewhere along the *Via Ignatia*, the great highway which connected the chief Macedonian towns with the seaport of Neapolis.

This departure of the apostle for Macedonia meant the abandonment of a previous arrangement, made with the Corinthians, it would seem, some time after 1 Corinthians was written, by which he was to go straight to Corinth from Asia, proceed from there to Macedonia, and afterwards return again through Corinth. He apologizes in 2 Cor. i. 15 ff. for this second change in his plans, of which they had by now become aware, explaining that it was not a mark of 'fickleness', the supposed defect in his character which some of the Corinthians had brought forward as the real explanation of his behaviour, but a proof of his genuine concern for their welfare, and of his determination, already expressed in the 'painful' letter, not to visit Corinth again till all was well in that distracted community.

We can imagine therefore the mixed feelings with which Paul awaited Titus' return in Macedonia, and the comfort which his report brought him. The worst, he learned, was now over. The majority of the Corinthians had shown great zeal on the apostle's behalf, and great sorrow at the pain which recent events had caused him (vii. 7). They had been genuinely grieved by the 'painful' letter, but their grief was not born of personal annoyance or wounded pride; it was not the sorrow of the world, but a godly sorrow productive of good works (vii. 9). The offending person had been duly dealt with, although the Corinthians had not been unanimous about the degree of the punishment that should be inflicted (ii. 6–8). The 'boasts' that the apostle had made to Titus to the effect that the mass of the Corinthians were really loyal at heart were proved to have been not in vain (vii. 14). Titus himself had returned with his affection for them greatly increased (vii. 15). The apostle was thus conscious at the moment of little but gratitude to God for the outcome of Titus' visit; and he pours forth his thankfulness in glowing words in the early chapters of 2 Corinthians. Sometimes indeed he almost writes as if the Corinthians were already perfect! 'I rejoice', he says, 'that I am in good spirits about you at every point' (vii. 16, Menzies' translation).

21

Such exuberant language was natural now that the strain of the previous months was over, and the storm-clouds seemed to have given way to glorious sunshine. But Paul knew well enough that in fact all was not so satisfactory as the reader might have been led to suppose if chapters i–vii had constituted the entire Epistle. There was still, for example, much slackness at Corinth in the matter of raising the quota for the Palestine relief fund; and, what was more serious, there were still false apostles at work trying to deflect the loyalty of the Corinthians from Paul to themselves. There had, it is true, been such a marked improvement that the apostle is now able to contemplate with equanimity the prospect of another visit to Corinth in the near future, but not before he has ventilated once again, and at some considerable length, the matter of the collection; and not before he has told the Corinthians precisely what he thinks about these 'super-apostles', and the fickleness shown by some whom he had reckoned as his friends in allowing themselves to be led astray by their specious arguments. The apostle had however the grace of tact, and he leaves his more severe warnings to the end!

The dominating purpose of 2 Corinthians is to prepare the readers for Paul's third visit. Let them, he urges, go forward along the way that Titus had told him they have already begun to tread. Titus has himself volunteered to return to Corinth to further the apostle's plans in the matter of the collection; and he is being accompanied by two other delegates of the churches (viii. 16–19). Paul himself will follow them in due course, but not immediately (see note on ix. 5). On this visit he will be ready, if necessary, to punish any who are still disobedient (x. 6); for he envisages the possibility of further evangelistic work in regions beyond Corinth, and he does not want to leave behind him the slumbering seeds of further disaffection (x. 15). Nor will he on this visit adjust his principles to suit those who may still be sneering at them. He will continue to refuse to be financially dependent on his converts (xii. 14). He will continue to wage war, as in the past, on the party-strife, the petty jealousies and the endless arguments that have such a disintegrating effect on Christian fellowship (xii. 20); and he will continue to be wholly uncompromising about immoral practices which degrade the standard of Christian life (xii. 21). Nor will he lightly pass over insinuations which may still be made against his own character; on the contrary, he will investigate them with the greatest possible care in the light of all the evidence available, and not hesitate to take severe measures to deal with the offenders, should such severity seem necessary (xiii. 1, 2). He is prepared to admit that on his last visit to Corinth, the 'painful' visit, he had shown what appeared to some to be weakness; but this, he assures them, will not happen again (xiii. 4). Before he comes, then, he calls upon each one of them to examine himself again and discover the faults that need to be rectified (xiii. 5), and by their elimination remove from him the disagreeable task of having to act with severity (xiii. 7).

If this fourth letter of Paul to the Corinthians had consisted merely of enthusiastic congratulations, there would have been a real danger that the Corinthians would slumber in self-contentment, as though no evils remained to be combated, and there were no further heights of Christian living to be won. This in itself, apart from other considerations which will be put forward in the next section, would seem sufficient explanation of the change of mood which differentiates the later chapters of the Epistle from the earlier. In fact, the way has been prepared for the appeal of the last four chapters, in which the apostle is pointing his readers to the future, by the expressions of gratitude and confidence found in the first nine chapters, in which he is for the most part concerned with the past and the present.

THE INTEGRITY OF 2 CORINTHIANS[1]

2 Corinthians has come down to us as a single Epistle. In no

[1] Some sentences in this chapter appeared in much the same form in my article on 'The Unity of 2 Corinthians', published in the *Expository Times*, Vol. XLVII, No. 2. I am grateful to the Editor for permission to make use of this material here.

MS is there any trace of a division at any point in the letter, or any variation in the arrangement of the material; and in no early Christian writer is there any suggestion that the document is composed of parts of different letters, or that it was not all written at one time to meet one particular situation. And yet, in spite of the complete absence of any external evidence in support of their views, many modern scholars have felt justified from internal evidence in concluding that it embodies fragments of one or more earlier letters written by the apostle to the Corinthians. It has become very fashionable to maintain that the last four chapters are not part of the letter which Paul wrote from Macedonia when he received the good news which Titus brought back from Corinth, but that they formed the closing portion of the 'painful' letter to which reference is made in 2 Cor. vii. 8. Many critics also suppose that the trenchant passage, vi. 14–vii. 1, is out of place in its present context, but belonged originally to the 'previous' letter to which the writer refers in 1 Cor. v. 9. It has also been held, though not so generally, that the section ii. 14–vii. 4 is alien to the context in which it is found, and interrupts what is otherwise a continuous sequence.[1]

Before considering the internal evidence which has led scholars to these conclusions, it may be well to ask whether in the light of our present knowledge about the way in which the Christians of the first and second centuries produced and published their 'books' it can be considered at all probable that dismembered fragments of earlier Epistles would become embodied in a single document.

[1] The further suggestion that chapter ix is part of a separate letter, possibly originally sent to the Christians of Achaia (see ix. 2) has not commended itself even to those who accept one or more of the other partition-theories; and it will not be considered here. A decisive answer to it was given by J. Moffatt who wrote: 'The unity of the situation presupposed in chapters viii and ix is too well-marked to justify any separation of the chapters from one another. In ix. 1 Paul is really explaining why he needs to say no more than he has said in viii. 24. Instead of being inconsistent with what precedes, ix. 1 clinches it, and ix. 5–7 simply shows that he felt a difficulty, not unnatural under the circumstances, about saying either too much or too little on the delicate topic of collecting money.' (J. Moffatt, *Introduction to the Literature of the New Testament*, p. 128. Third Edition, 1918.)

It can be regarded as fairly certain that the canonical First Epistle to the Corinthians passed into general circulation somewhat earlier than the Second. Clement of Rome in his letter to the Corinthians written in 96, the earliest extant non-canonical Christian writing, bids them 'take up the Epistle of the blessed Paul', and makes several quotations from the First Epistle as if this was the only Epistle to the Corinthians known to him, though, as has often been pointed out, the contents of 2 Corinthians would have been by no means irrelevant to the subject of his own exhortation. It can be reasonably deduced from this that the Second Epistle, not being known in Rome at the end of the first century, was slower in passing into circulation than the First. It can be admitted at the outset of our discussion that if 2 Corinthians was in circulation somewhat late, there would have been time for some of Paul's earlier letters to Corinth to have suffered disintegration through neglect, and for the later editing of such fragments as happened to survive, so that they came to form the composite document known to us as 2 Corinthians. In the cautious words of A. Robertson 'the comparatively late appearance of 2 Corinthians in the stream of attestation is perhaps compatible with some process of editing on the part of the Corinthian church before it was copied for public reading and imparted to other churches'. And, as the same writer goes on to say, 'this would be easier to suppose, if the autographs were written on leaves or tablets rather than on rolls'.[1]

It is however extremely unlikely that any but the shortest of Paul's Epistles, such as the Epistle to Philemon, was originally written on separate sheets of papyrus, unfolded or unfastened, which might easily have become misplaced or lost. And although, as C. H. Roberts has recently pointed out in a very important monograph 'The Codex'[2], 'so universal is the use of the codex by Christians in the second century that the beginnings of this process must be taken back well into the

[1] Hastings, *Dictionary of the Bible*, Vol. I, p. 497 (T. and T. Clark, 1898).
[2] Published in *The Proceedings of the British Academy*, Vol. XL (Geoffrey Cumberlege, 1956).

first century', we have no evidence for supposing that the codex form of book was used by Christians in Asia for correspondence in the life-time of Paul. The papyrus roll would seem to have been almost universally used for letters of any length or importance. Writing tablets constructed either of pieces of wood, the centre of which had been hollowed and covered with wax to form a surface for writing, or of strips of leather held together by a clasp or by strings passed through pierced holes, were used in later Greece, in C. H. Robert's words, 'for anything of an impermanent nature—letters, bills, school exercises, memoranda, a writer's first draft'. It may very well be that the reference in 2 Tim. iv. 13 'especially the parchments' refers to Paul's own note-books constructed in this way. But for larger letters, which had to be conveyed by hand for a considerable distance, and which Paul intended to be read in public and on more than one occasion, we may be almost certain that the papyrus roll was used.

As long as the various letters of Paul to the Corinthians existed on papyrus rolls, it is unlikely that they would have suffered the kind of damage that is necessary for the supposition that only fragments of them (though curiously enough rather neat and tidy fragments) were in existence, when the hypothetical editor undertook his work of salvage and constructed our 2 Corinthians. It is much more probable that distintegration into loose sheets, capable of being edited in a not wholly unconvincing manner, if it happened at all, happened after the letters had been copied in codex or 'book' form. We do not know why the Christians used the papyrus codex far earlier than secular publishers. But we may reasonably conjecture that apart from purely practical considerations such as economy of space, convenience of transport, and greater ease of reference, the dominant reason was that these works which by being copied into codices were being given a greater dignity of format, were *already* regarded as possessing a high degree of authority. And it is surely very difficult to believe that once this authority was generally recognized, and this may have happened very early, the recipients of Paul's letters would treat them with such lack of care that they would be allowed literally to fall to pieces. Some of Paul's letters, it may well be, were never copied in codex form, and may have been deliberately destroyed because they were never intended for wider circulation. This we believe to have been the case with both the 'previous' and the 'painful' letters. As Dibelius has truly said, 'it was by no means in the interest of the church that the "painful" letter should be published abroad, and hence, after the reconciliation between the Corinthians and Paul, it could have been regarded as wiped out; thus we need not be surprised that it is lacking in the collection of the Pauline letters.' And with regard to the 'previous' letter Dibelius asserts, 'it was misunderstood, just because it was not quite clear; it was then corrected and finally superseded by the canonical First Epistle.'[1] But once the apostle's letters were considered valuable enough to copy into codices they would, we may suppose, not only be in constant use but also carefully treasured.

It is therefore very difficult, if not impossible, to accept the following conclusion of C. L. Mitton, based on the unproved assumption that there are 'demonstrable dislocations' to be found in all the extant copies of 2 Corinthians. 'These features of the letters suggest that they have not been individually treasured and preserved with the utmost care, but rather that they have been treated with a measure of indifference and neglect, with the result that the individual sheets had disintegrated, and it was left to a collector to rearrange them as best he could. His interest would be spiritual truth and not historical and literary accuracy, and so the errors in arrangement would be less noticeable to him than to us.'[2]

On the other hand, if we are to assume that the letters, fragments from which are supposed to be present in our 2 Corinthians, existed undamaged and *in toto* when an imaginary

---

[1] Martin Dibelius, *A Fresh Approach to the New Testament and Early Christian Literature*, p. 154 (Ivor Nicholson and Watson, 1936).

[2] C. L. Mitton, *The Formation of the Pauline Corpus of Letters*, p. 26 (Epworth Press, 1955).

editor, using what we should call today 'scissors-and-paste' methods, produced the amalgam of our present document, we are compelled to ask certain pertinent questions, to which there are no satisfactory answers. By what authority did such an editor act? Upon what principles did he go to work? Why, for example, should he have substituted the closing portion of the 'painful' letter for the closing portion of the final letter? The reason often suggested for this is that the earlier sections of the former contained personal references to the offender at Corinth, which the Corinthians did not think it wise to publish to the outside world, particularly in his lifetime. But we are then forced to ask, why should the closing portion of the 'painful' letter, if it was necessary to destroy its earlier sections, not have been attached to the *end* of the letter of which 2 Cor. i–ix is the beginning, instead of being added after chapter ix? Why moreover should he have deleted from the 'painful' letter the essential matter referred to in 2 Cor. ii and vii? And why, finally, should he have inserted the fragment from the 'previous' letter in a context which advocates of the partition-theory are agreed in finding highly unsuitable? It is, in fact, very difficult to envisage either the historical situation in which the supposed dislocations may be supposed to have arisen, or the literary process by which the resultant fragments came to be edited and preserved. Such a hypothesis, unsupported as it is by the entire textual tradition, ought only to be resorted to if the internal evidence is overwhelmingly strong. To a consideration of that evidence we now turn our attention.

The supposition that the section ii. 14–vii. 4 is a fragment from another letter has really very little to support it. Dr. Mitton, however, writes with confidence: 'A further dislocation is almost certainly to be found at 2 Cor. ii. 14. In the preceding verses, in self-explanation, Paul is giving a careful account of his actions. He has told of the restless anxiety for Titus' return from Corinth which kept him from patiently awaiting his arrival at Troas, and then drove him on into Macedonia in hope of meeting Titus the sooner. Then the urgent narrative breaks off, to be resumed at vii. 5 with a description of harassing trouble in Macedonia and at last the relief and joy of Titus' arrival and the good news he brought. In Paul's original letter, vii. 5 would follow ii. 13, and the intervening verses may be regarded as a further instance of an insertion from another Pauline letter.'[1] We may not unreasonably retort that the 'urgent narrative breaks off' for an even greater urgency, the desire of the apostle to thank God for the wonderful privilege and the astonishing results of his ministry, a subject which never ceased to fill him with gratitude and awe. Digressions are very common in Paul's letters; and in a document such as 2 Corinthians, written at the close of a long period of strain and tension, it is not surprising that this somewhat longer digression should be found.

The theory that the passage vi. 14–vii. 1 belongs to the 'previous' letter is based on the consideration that in its present position it not only interrupts the context, but brings in a set of ideas said to be essentially alien to it. Paul at this point of the letter is opening his heart in a very intimate manner to the Corinthians, appealing to them with no little tenderness to make a real and genuine response to him, and then he suddenly seems to address them as though they were still unconverted and engrossed in heathenism. What a tactless way, it is said, to go to work! How out of keeping with the playful touch of vi. 13, 'I speak as unto my children'! How much more intelligible is the language of this passage, if it formed part of the letter dealing specifically with a grievous sin, the 'previous' letter, which Paul expressly says he wrote to the Corinthians to warn them to have nothing to do with fornicators (see 1 Cor. v. 9). Does not this latter reference throw a flood of light on the kind of language used in vi. 14–vii. 1? 'What concord hath Christ with Belial? . . . What agreement hath the temple of God with idols? . . . Come out from among them, and be ye separate, saith the Lord, and touch not the unclean thing. . . . Let us cleanse ourselves from all filthiness of the flesh!' Moreover, it is pointed out that, if this section is omitted from its present context, no ugly hiatus is caused, for Paul continues in

[1] *Op. cit.*, p. 26.

vii. 2 with the same subject as that with which he was dealing in vi. 13, and in very similar language.

But it is equally possible that the similarity of the language of vii. 2 and vi. 13 is an indication that the writer himself is conscious that, having left his main theme for the moment, he is now picking it up again. It would be very natural, moreover, for one so accustomed to preaching to the heathen to use on occasions the same type of language, even when he was dictating a letter to be read by a congregation of converted men and women. The Corinthian letters were written in the bustle and turmoil of a strenuous missionary career by one who could never for a moment forget the reality or the potency of the pagan forces with which the young Christian communities were surrounded. And after the urgent reminder given by him in v. 10 that we must all appear before the judgment seat of Christ, and the passionate appeal in vi. 1, 2 to remember that the day of grace, now present, will not last for ever, the exhortation that begins in vi. 14 cannot be considered either incongruous or irrelevant. Finally, do not the words 'I have said before' (vii. 3) suggest that Paul is deliberately referring back to what he has said in vi. 11–13 after what he is conscious to have been a somewhat abrupt diversion?

The conjecture that the last four chapters of 2 Corinthians formed the closing section of the 'painful' letter is of a somewhat different character from the supposed interpolation we have just been considering. Here we are confronted not by a temporary change of tone extending over a few verses, but by one which colours a large and important section of the Epistle. To the advocates of the partition-theory it seems psychologically incredible that the same man who wrote the first nine chapters should have followed them in the same letter by chapters x–xiii. In the latter chapters, it is pointed out, Paul is writing mainly in self-defence. He is not at all sure whether he has the confidence of his readers or not. He threatens that if he comes to visit them again he will not spare them. He is anxious and nervous, and not sure whether his

quarrel with the Corinthians is really over. In the earlier
chapters, on the other hand, the storm-clouds have clearly
lifted. All is easy and happy. The apostle is full of confidence.
The Corinthians have been fully tested and not found wanting.
In everything he can wax bold concerning them. Joy, comfort
and relief—these, it is said, are clearly the marks of the
opening chapters, as surely as doubt and hesitation characterize the more apologetic and aggressive closing passages.

That there is a marked change of tone at the beginning of
chapter x is evident to every reader of the letter. It is, however,
very easy to exaggerate it; and it is very doubtful whether in
itself it is sufficient to warrant the theory that the closing
chapters belong to another letter, or to justify such a verdict,
for example, as that of Rendall who wrote 'Tradition has
handed down 2 Corinthians as a complete and entire whole.
In so doing it has robbed it of much of its interpretative value'.
Very different, but it would seem nearer the truth, is the
impression made by the Epistle on R. A. Knox. 'It has been
suggested', he writes, 'that chapters x–xiii, with their tone of
disappointment and strong expostulation, do not really fit on
to the earlier chapters of the Epistle which breathe a spirit of
confidence and approval, especially chapter vii. But the difficulty, so stated, is stated wrongly. What is really curious is that
chapters vii–ix, which breathe a spirit of confidence and
approval, should have been sandwiched in where they are; *all*
the rest of the Epistle is disappointment and expostulation. It
looks as if Paul had written his first nine chapters, ending up
on a quiet note with the collection (cf. 1 Cor. xvi), and then
some fresh access of misgiving, or perhaps some fresh piece of
news had produced the splendid outburst of chapters x–xiii.'[1]
Even if this judgment errs a little in the opposite direction, it at
least shows how different readers, equally intelligent and
equally versed in literary criticism, are capable of coming to
very different conclusions about the harmony or lack of
harmony between the earlier and later sections of this Epistle.

[1] *A New Testament Commentary for English Readers*, Vol. ii, p. 175 (Burns,
Oates and Washbourne, 1954).

The opening words of 2 Cor. x, 'Now I Paul myself beseech you by the meekness and gentleness of Christ', seem to suggest that the writer is conscious that he is going to write in a somewhat different strain from the earlier chapters, and to speak with special emphasis (cf. Gal. v. 2). And he has a motive for so doing. He does not want the Corinthians to imagine that, now that they have dealt with the offender, there is no danger of further lapses on their part. He has opened his heart to them in gratitude for their loyalty; but the seeds of disunion may still be slumbering in many hearts, ready to break into life again at the next onslaught of the 'false apostles', whose efforts are uncompromising and untiring. There must be no living in a fool's paradise, unaware of the dangers lying ahead. The Corinthians must make up their minds, *all* of them, whether Paul is really their apostle or not. There must be no longer any kind of hesitation about this. It is as their apostle by divine commission that he is going to visit them once again, claiming the allegiance that is his due. Hence it is natural that before he brings to a close the letter, which is to pave the way for that visit, he should vindicate once again his apostolic authority and show his superiority to other false apostles.

But there is another question worth asking in considering the unity of this Epistle. Do the closing chapters read as though they were part of the 'painful' letter, which the apostle himself tells us was written with tears, and which he had some regrets at having written? Why should he have regretted writing, for example, about his authority as an apostle, or the glory of his sufferings as a minister of Christ? Were not these the themes upon which he very often and quite unashamedly touched in writing to his converts? Did it really cost him tears to tell the Corinthians that all things were for their edification (xii. 19), or that he was ready to spend and be spent out on their behalf (xii. 15)? Is the tone of chapters x–xiii, in a word, quite as severe as at a first reading it might appear to be? There is surely a playful strain also running through these chapters, which tends to modify not a little the sharpness of the language, and makes us hesitate before coming to the conclusion that they belong to the 'painful' letter, written, we may believe, in a very different mood. The reference to his 'speaking as a fool'; the whole manner in which the visions are described at the beginning of chapter xii; the very description of the false apostles as 'the superlative apostles' (xii. 11); the request 'to be forgiven this wrong' in reference to the fact that the apostle had not lived at the expense of the Corinthian church; and the words 'being crafty, I caught you with guile' (xii. 16)—these are all signs that the writer is not writing, somewhat at white heat, a letter truly described as a 'painful' letter, but that he is giving a gentle but firm warning to the Corinthians that he will not tolerate any further slipping back into disloyalty.

It is urged, however, by those who regard 2 Corinthians as a series of disconnected fragments, that not merely is the general difference in tone between the early and the later chapters great enough to warrant the assumption that they belong to different letters, but that there are definite references in the earlier chapters to statements in the later ones, thus proving that chapters i–ix were written subsequently to chapters x–xiii. The words in ii. 3 'I wrote this same unto you, lest, when I came, I should have sorrow' are said to be a reference to xiii. 10, 'Therefore I write these things being absent, lest being present I should use sharpness.' The readiness of the apostle 'to revenge all disobedience, when your obedience is fulfilled', found in x. 6, is said to be previous to his statement in ii. 9, 'For to this end also did I write, that I might know the proof of you, whether ye be obedient in all things.' Finally, the threat voiced in xiii. 2, 'If I come again, I will not spare' antedates, it is said, the statement of i. 23, 'To spare you I came not as yet unto Corinth.' But these two sets of passages make excellent sense precisely where they stand. The group from the earlier part of the Epistle contain explanations why the apostle abandoned a proposed visit to Corinth, and wrote the 'painful' letter instead; while the latter group refer to a forthcoming visit which took place subsequently to the writing of 2 Corinthians and is mentioned in passing in Acts xx. 2. When, moreover, it is suggested that the references to self-commendation in iii. 1 and v. 12 are denials on the part of the apostle that he is going to start doing all over again what his readers know that he has already done in chapters x–xiii, it may well be replied that in *both* parts of the Epistle Paul is careful to state he never indulges in the kind of self-commendation with which his opponents at Corinth have made the Corinthians so familiar (cf. iii. 1 and x. 16).

It would seem to be perfectly possible to trace sufficient unity of thought in the document as it stands at least to make it intelligible. The Epistle, as Menzies rightly says, 'is all about a proposed visit'. This visit the apostle is anxious to make a real success. Everything must go well on his third appearance in Corinth. The Corinthians must have their collection for the poor saints ready, and must be unanimous in their loyalty to himself. There is one thing that the apostle fears, and his fear reveals itself in the earlier as well as in the later chapters, and that is that the false apostles at Corinth, whose jibes about himself he refers to as early in the letter as i. 17 and iv. 2, may make a further attempt, before he arrives, to seduce the Corinthians from their loyalty. 'All through the earlier chapters', as R. A. Knox rightly says, 'Paul shows definite signs of uneasiness, expostulating with his converts, e.g. in vi. 11–18, and hinting in v. 20 and vi. 1 that he is delivering an ultimatum. It is of course possible that after writing i–ix he received fresh news from Corinth which exposed a new state of affairs. But it is perhaps more probable that Titus had come back from his mission with a mixed budget of news. . . . The apostle still had his critics who were pursuing him with vague charges of inconsistency and weakness; perhaps too (see vi. 11–18) the Corinthians were still flirting with idolatry in defiance of 1 Cor. viii–x.'[1]

There is another possible reference to the false apostles at Corinth in ii. 17, 'We are not as many, which corrupt the word of God', particularly if the reading *hoi loipoi*, 'the rest' (i.e. the rest of those known to you Corinthians) is adopted in place of

[1] *Op. cit.*, p. 195.

hoi polloi, 'the many'. Another very convincing argument for the unity of the Epistle is to be found in a comparison of viii. 6 and xii. 18. In the former of these passages, the delegates from the churches are introduced to the Corinthians; in the latter, it is assumed that the Corinthians have already been informed about them (see commentary on xii. 18).

A. Robertson ended his discussion on the integrity of 2 Corinthians in the article from which we have already quoted with the words, 'We believe that a patient and circumspect exegesis will gradually dissolve the arguments, at first sight very tempting, for the segregation of chapters x-xiii, and even perhaps of vi. 14–vii. 1.' It would seem that since the writing of those words in the closing years of the last century no further arguments have been adduced of sufficient weight to discredit the confidence they express. It is therefore our duty to approach the Second Epistle to the Corinthians as a unity, and to attempt to 'see it steadily and see it whole'.

ANALYSIS

I. GREETING AND THANKSGIVING (i. 1–11).

   a. The address and salutation (i. 1, 2).
   b. Divine consolation (i. 3–7).
   c. The trouble in Asia (i. 8–11).

II. PAUL DEFENDS HIS INTEGRITY (i. 12–ii. 11).

   a. Paul's sincerity (i. 12–14).
   b. Paul not guilty of fickleness (i. 15–22).
   c. Reasons for Paul's change of plans (i. 23–ii. 4).
   d. The treatment of the offender (ii. 5–11).

III. PAUL'S APOSTOLIC MINISTRY (ii. 12–vi. 10).

   a. Paul's recent journey to Macedonia (ii. 12, 13).
   b. Paul's thanksgiving for his share in Christ's triumphs (ii. 14–17).
   c. Letters testimonial (iii. 1–3).
   d. The Old and New Covenants (iii. 4–18).
   e. The 'openness' of the apostolic ministry (iv. 1–6).
   f. The contrast between the message and the messenger (iv. 7–15).
   g. Outward decline and inward renewal (iv. 16–18).
   h. The Christian hope (v. 1–10).
   i. The constraining love of Christ (v. 11–15).
   j. The new creation (v. 16, 17).
   k. The ministry of reconciliation (v. 18–21).
   l. Paul's experiences as a herald of salvation (vi. 1–10).

IV. AN APPEAL FOR LARGE-HEARTEDNESS AND CONSISTENCY (vi. 11–vii. 3).

V. PAUL'S COMFORT AT THE NEWS BROUGHT BY TITUS (vii. 4–16).

VI. THE COLLECTION FOR THE CHRISTIAN POOR IN JUDAEA (viii. 1–ix. 15).

   a. The example of the Macedonians (viii. 1–7).
   b. The supreme motive for Christian giving (viii. 8–15).
   c. The delegates of the churches (viii. 16–ix. 5).
   d. The blessings that await the generous (ix. 6–15).

VII. PAUL'S APOSTOLIC AUTHORITY (x. 1–xiii. 10).

    a. The weapons of his warfare (x. 1–6).
    b. Paul's consistency (x. 7–11).
    c. Paul's appointed sphere of service (x. 12–18).
    d. Paul's claims on the Corinthians' loyalty (xi. 1–6).
    e. Paul's pride in being self-sufficient (xi. 7–12).
    f. The real nature of Paul's opponents (xi. 13–15).
    g. Paul's credentials and experiences (xi. 16–33).
    h. Paul's visions and thorn in the flesh (xii. 1–10).
    i. Paul's behaviour at Corinth on previous visits (xii. 11–13).
    j. Paul's behaviour on his proposed visit (xii. 14–21).
    k. Paul's determination to restore discipline at Corinth (xiii. 1–10).

VIII. CONCLUSION (xiii. 11–14).

COMMENTARY

I. GREETING AND THANKSGIVING (i. 1–11)

a. The address and salutation (i. 1, 2)

1, 2. In 1 Corinthians Sosthenes is associated with Paul in the opening address, but there is no mention of Timothy. It would appear from 1 Cor. iv. 17 that Timothy had already been sent to Corinth by the time 1 Corinthians was written; and it may be assumed from 1 Cor. xvi. 10 that Paul was uncertain whether Timothy or the Epistle would reach Corinth first. We have no record of the success or failure of Timothy's mission; but, as Titus seems to have superseded him as Paul's emissary to Corinth between the writing of 1 and 2 Corinthians, it may well be that the anxiety felt about him by the apostle which finds expression in 1 Cor. xvi. 10 was justified, and that Timothy rejoined him at Ephesus with nothing to report but failure. Presumably he moved on with the apostle to Troas and into Macedonia (see 2 Cor. ii. 12, 13), and he sends his greetings to the Corinthians along with those of Paul in the opening verse of this Epistle.

It is clear that both the canonical Epistles to the Corinthians were intended by their author to be read at other places besides Corinth. In 1 Corinthians not only is the church of God at Corinth addressed but 'all that call upon the name of our Lord Jesus Christ in every place'; and here *the saints which are in all Achaia* are coupled with the local church. (For the meaning of *Achaia* see note on ix. 2.) We know from Acts xvii. 34 that there were Christians at Athens, and from Rom. xvi. 1 that there was a church at Cenchrea, to mention two of the towns that were situated in the district of Achaia. Paul was conscious that his written words were significant for the whole Church of God, and not merely for the particular local churches at which they were first delivered.[1] It is probable that these local churches kept copies of his letters forwarded to them by their neighbours, and so came to possess small collections of their own. These would continue to be read out at their gatherings for worship along with the Old Testament Scriptures, containing, as they did, a divine message mediated through the apostle.

For the significance of Paul's opening greeting *grace . . . and peace* see the *Tyndale Commentary on Thessalonians*, pp. 32, 33.

b. Divine consolation (i. 3–7)

3. Instead of passing on at once after the salutation to a thanksgiving for the spiritual progress of his readers, as was his custom, Paul offers praise for wonderful mercies recently vouchsafed to himself. The words *Blessed . . . Christ* are found again in exactly the same form in 1 Pet. i. 3. It is therefore odd that the AV translation here should be *God, even the Father*, and in the Petrine passage 'the God and Father'. While both translations are possible, the latter, found in both places in RV, is a more natural rendering of the Greek. This majestic benediction contains profound theological truths. These have been well summarized by E. G. Selwyn. 'God is now revealed and known . . . not as God only, but as God revealed in relation to His only begotten Son, and not as His Father only but also as His God, for the incarnation does not exhaust God's manifestation of Himself. And the Son is described in three ways; in relationship to us (our *Lord*); in His Person (*Jesus*); and in His divinely-promised and world-wide office (*Christ*)'.[2]

The expression *the Father of mercies* is a Hebrew way of saying 'the all-merciful Father'. As a collect in the Book of Common Prayer expresses it, His 'nature and property is ever to have mercy and to forgive'. By designating Him further *the God of all*

---

[1] *Cf.* the remark of the writer of the Muratorian Fragment (a list of canonical books *c.* 170). 'Paul writes by name to seven churches; . . . although there is a second to the Thessalonians and Corinthians, yet one Church is recognized as being spread over the entire world.'

[2] *The First Epistle of Peter*, p. 122 (Macmillan, 1946).

comfort the apostle affirms that He is the source of encouragement and consolation to believers under all circumstances. The word translated *comfort* in verses 3 and 4 is translated *consolation* in verses 5, 6 and 7. RV and RSV rightly retain *comfort* throughout; and this word perhaps better than any other conveys the double meaning of 'encouragement' and 'consolation' inherent in the Greek word *paraclēsis*.

4. When Paul speaks of God as *the God of all comfort* he is speaking of something he has himself experienced, for the plural *us* refers primarily, though not exclusively, to himself.[1] He can testify that on every occasion when he has been in *tribulation* (for such would seem to be the implication of the Greek *epi pasē thlipsei*) he has been so sustained and strengthened by the hand of God that he has been able not merely to endure it but to derive blessings from it. Not the least of these blessings is the ability that such experiences have given him to extend to others in their hour of trouble a sympathy born of the divine sympathy he himself has been privileged to receive. 'Of the many solutions given in Scripture of the mystery of pain', Menzies comments, 'this is not the least notable; the sufferer who feels that his sufferings equip him as a missionary of comfort to others will feel that they are well-explained.'

5. This ministry of comforting others is always possible for the apostle, because however great and frequent his own sufferings may be, the divine comfort is always fully sufficient for the occasion. He can call his sufferings *the sufferings of Christ*, because as a man united with Christ, and as a Christian missionary, he is called upon to endure the same kind of sufferings as Christ Himself endured. Jesus told His apostles that they would have to drink of His cup and be baptized with the baptism He was baptized with (see Mt. xx. 23). But, just as Christ suffered for the joy that was set before Him, so His servants, who are united with Him in suffering, are also

---

[1] This phenomenon is found frequently in this Epistle.

privileged to enjoy the consolation which He shares with them. They would not have to undergo the kind of suffering that they do if they were not 'men in Christ'; but it is because they are 'men in Christ' that they are the recipients of divine comfort.

6, 7. A comparison of AV and RV reveals that there is considerable variation in the MSS in the order in which the several clauses in these two verses are arranged. The general sense however remains the same, whichever order we adopt. The main idea is clear; it is well expressed in Hodge's simple summary 'Whether we be afflicted, it is for your good; or whether we be comforted, it is for your good'. The Corinthians, seeing the nobility of the apostle's conduct under suffering, are encouraged when called upon to suffer themselves; this makes his own sufferings supremely worth while. And, similarly, as the comfort that he experiences in his own sufferings can be passed on by him to them in their hour of trouble, their sufferings are rendered more endurable, and they can face the future without dismay, conscious that they are treading the way of salvation.

c. The trouble in Asia (i. 8–11)

8. Having first drawn his readers' attention to the truth expressed in the two previous verses, Paul now reminds them of the very serious nature of his recent sufferings *in Asia* (i.e. proconsular Asia). He had been *pressed out of measure* (RV 'weighed down exceedingly' like a beast of burden crushed beneath too heavy a load) and beyond his powers of endurance, so that he regarded immediate death as a certainty. By *trouble* (RV 'affliction') it is at first sight natural to suppose that Paul is referring to the uproar at Ephesus described in Acts xix. 23–41. But there is no suggestion in that passage that Paul was in any acute personal danger on that occasion; and the narrative seems to imply that he was able to leave Ephesus immediately the uproar ceased (see xx. 1). It is difficult to think that Luke would have omitted any reference to Paul's *trouble* at this time if it had been as serious as the apostle here asserts.

It may be that Paul is recalling some severe illness. This, as R. A. Knox points out, would help to explain the rather mysterious language of verse 9. *We had the sentence* (RV rightly 'answer') *of death in ourselves.* It is often thought that these words imply that Paul had a presentiment that he was going to lose his life at the hands of others. But, as Knox reminds us, no parallel has been adduced for such a curious turn of expression. On the other hand, if he was sick unto death, he may well have felt *in himself* the signs of mortality. Nevertheless, *trouble* (Gk. *thlipsis*) seems a rather strange word to use of serious illness. Rendall refers the *trouble* to 'the anguish of spirit caused by the revolt and estrangement of Paul's Corinthian converts', of which he does not hesitate to remind them, even though all is now well; but, as Plummer remarks, 'the language of verses 8 to 10 seems too strong for the reception of such news', however painful it may have been. In the absence of any precise information a form of persecution due to mob-violence, somewhere in Asia but not necessarily at Ephesus, is probably the best conjecture we can make.

9. Whatever the exact nature of the *trouble* may have been— when Paul asked himself at the time what the issue would be, the 'answer' he found present in his mind was '*death*'. But, when he looked back on the hours when he had stood at death's door, he knew that he had been allowed in the providence of God to go through that terrible experience, that he might be brought to a full recognition of his own utter helplessness and, abandoning all self-confidence, learn to *trust . . . in God which raiseth the dead.*

10, 11. God is pre-eminently the God of resurrection. He raised Jesus from the dead; He raises men up from the death of sin to a life of righteousness; and He will raise mankind in the final general resurrection. Wholly in keeping with this unique attribute of His nature, God rescued Paul on that memorable

43

occasion in Asia from *so great a death* (i.e. from a death that seemed so terrible and so inevitable). Nothing but the hand of God could have effected such a deliverance. The reading followed by AV *and doth deliver* might imply that the danger is not yet past. The better attested reading, adopted by RV, gives the sense *and will deliver*; and it may well be that the future tense was altered by later scribes to the present in view of the occurrence of another future in the following clause.

As the word *that* should almost certainly be omitted, as in our most ancient authorities including P.46 and B, it would seem best to construe the words *in whom we trust* with the preceding words giving the sense 'And He will deliver us again, He in whom we trust': or, in the more accurate translation of RV, He 'on whom we have set our hope'. In this case, the closing words of verse 10 will begin a new sentence running on into verse 11, the sense being 'And indeed (translating *kai* which is untranslated in AV) *he will yet deliver us, ye also helping together by prayer*'.

There is no limit to the power of intercessory prayer; and though the display of God's mercy does not depend upon it, we may be sure that He desires nothing more than that His people should be united in mutual intercession offered in the name of His Son. When such prayer is answered, it results in an outburst of praise and thanksgiving which redounds greatly to God's glory. The sense of AV and RV in verse 11 seems to be, that if *many persons* have prayed for *the gift bestowed upon* the apostles by God, *thanks* will *be given by many* on their behalf. But, as the word translated *persons* means literally *faces*, and as the expression *by the means of many persons* could equally well be connected with the giving of thanks as with *the gift bestowed*, the sense of the last part of the verse may well be that given in the fine translation of W. G. Rutherford, 'that there may be a sea of upturned faces as a widespread thanksgiving goes up to God on our behalf for the gracious act which He has done for us'.[1]

---

[1] *St. Paul's Epistles to the Thessalonians and to the Corinthians. A New Translation* (Macmillan, 1908).

II. PAUL DEFENDS HIS INTEGRITY (i. 12–ii. 11)

a. Paul's sincerity (i. 12–14)

12. Paul can appeal for this cooperation of the Corinthians in prayer, because, contrary to what his opponents are saying about him, he discharges the duties of his apostleship with utter sincerity. The word translated *rejoicing*, *kauchēsis*, is more accurately rendered in RV by 'glorying' and in RSV by 'boast'. Paul does not hesitate to be proud that his conscience bears him witness that his general behaviour, more particularly in his dealings with the Corinthians, has been characterized by *simplicity and godly sincerity*. The better attested reading *hagiotēti* 'holiness' instead of *haplotēti simplicity* is adopted by RV and RSV. The change from the former to the latter, if not due to an error in copying, may have arisen because *simplicity* seemed a more suitable accompaniment of *sincerity*. The noun 'holiness', moreover, is not found elsewhere in the Pauline Epistles, while there are some six or seven occurrences of *simplicity*.

The derivation of the word *eilikrinia*, translated here and in ii. 17 by *sincerity*, is uncertain. It may refer to the cleansing process of rolling and shaking in a sieve, so that what is purged and winnowed in this way may be regarded as unadulterated (cf. the only other mention of the word by Paul in 1 Cor. v. 8). Or it may denote what is found to be unstained when examined in the sunlight. This latter connotation would convey the suggestion in this passage that Paul's character would stand the test of the searching gaze of God. T. H. Green, accordingly, translated the word in the present passage 'perfect openness to God'.

As a minister of Christ Paul does not act *with fleshly wisdom*, i.e. with the shrewdness and artfulness of a man prompted by motives of self-interest and self-aggrandizement. On the contrary, he is guided and controlled *by the grace of God*. The thought of what God in His condescending love has done for him and all mankind in the redeeming work of Christ is the dominating factor in his life.[1]

[1] See further in this connection the author's sermon on 'The Spirit of Christian Ethics' in *The Narrow Way* (Inter-Varsity Fellowship, 1952).

13, 14. It is clear that Paul had been accused by his opponents of being particularly insincere in his letters. 'He means something different', they said 'from what he actually writes.' In reply, the apostle insists that his letter-writing has the same mark of sincerity as the rest of his conduct. He writes nothing but what his readers can read and understand (see RSV). There are no innuendos or reservations. If the way the following clauses are grouped in AV and RV is correct, Paul goes on to express the hope that this will always be the case *even to the end*. A better understanding of the passage is perhaps obtained if a full-stop is placed after *what ye read or acknowledge*, if the clause *that we are your rejoicing* is construed as the object of *I trust ye shall acknowledge*, and if *to the end* (*heōs telous*) is given the more probable meaning 'completely'. The sense that emerges from such a rearrangement is that Paul recognizes that the Corinthians' understanding of him at present is *in part*, but he hopes that they will come to apprehend completely that they can be as proud of him as he can be of them *in the day of the Lord Jesus*. When Christ appears as Judge and the secrets of all hearts are disclosed, Paul's hope is that they will each have cause to be proud of the other (see RSV).

b. Paul not guilty of fickleness (i. 15–22)

15, 16. In I Cor. xvi. 5 Paul informed the Corinthians that he proposed to visit them after he had passed through Macedonia. In these two verses he refers to another plan, made it would seem *after* the writing of I Corinthians, and prompted by the consideration that the Corinthians were well-disposed towards him. He would cross straight over to Corinth, and after visiting Macedonia return to Corinth again, whence he hoped *to be brought on his way*, i.e. 'given a good send-off', *toward Judaea*. This would enable the Corinthians to have *a second benefit*, i.e. the benefit of seeing him twice. B reads *charan*, 'joy', instead of *charin, benefit*; and this reading is adopted by RSV 'a double pleasure'.

This revised plan must have been communicated to the Corinthians; and they must also have been informed of his subsequent decision to abandon it, for he now feels obliged to defend himself against the charge of fickleness which had been brought against him at Corinth when the news became known that he had twice changed his mind. The word *proteron*, translated *before*, could mean 'originally', and be construed with *I was minded* with the sense 'I originally intended'; but more probably it should be given the meaning 'first' and taken closely with 'to you'. So RSV 'I wanted to come to you first', i.e. before going to Macedonia.

17. Having decided upon this plan for a double visit, was he guilty, Paul now asks rhetorically, of *lightness* (RV 'fickleness') in abandoning it? Was it, moreover, his usual practice to plan *according to the flesh*, i.e. as an ordinary man of the world guided by trivial or purely selfish considerations, so that he could say 'Yes, Yes' and then follow it almost at once with 'No, No'? The presence in the original of the definite article before *lightness*, and also before 'Yes, Yes' and 'No, No' probably indicates that Paul is quoting what is being said about him at Corinth (so RV 'the yea yea and the nay nay'). Such is the sense of both AV and RV. The RSV translation gives a different, but equally possible, meaning of Paul's first question, 'Was I vacillating when I wanted to do this?'

18. The very thought that such light-heartedness in his dealings with his converts was a possibility, however remote, is so utterly abhorrent to Paul, that he now makes a solemn assertion. As surely *as God is true*, he affirms, his own words to the Corinthians, whether conveying news of his own personal plans or transmitting to them the sublime truths of the gospel, are *not* the utterances of a vacillator who says 'Yes' and 'No' almost in the same breath.

19. Paul could never be a 'Yes and No' man, for the *Jesus* preached by him at Corinth, and also by Silvanus and Timothy, was not a merely human figure subject to the uncertainty, the indecision, and the inconsistency that characterize the behaviour of ordinary men and women. He was *the Son of God*, Himself the absolute Truth. He was also the *Christ*, who in His

47

own Person and work brought to its glorious climax the entire previous revelation made by God to His people. Never could *He* be designated a 'Yes and No' person, for 'in him', as RSV translates, 'it is always Yes'. Never did He hesitate to give an unqualified assent to all that His Father demanded of Him.

20. Paul is emphatic that *all the promises of God* made in earlier days to patriarchs and prophets found their fulfilment in Christ. He would seem to be thinking not merely of such direct predictions of incidents in the life of Jesus as are noted by the four Evangelists, but also of such promises as 'the just shall live by faith' (Hab. ii. 4); 'in thy seed shall all the nations of the earth be blessed' (Gn. xxii. 18); and 'he will swallow up death in victory' (Is. xxv. 8).

Instead of the second *in him* the most ancient MSS have 'wherefore also through him' (RV). It is, in other words, because Christ is the divine 'Yes' or 'Amen' (these two words having so similar a meaning that they are found in apposition in Rev. i. 7), that Christians are moved to say 'Amen', i.e. 'Yes indeed', 'This is the truth', when they are engaged in worship. And, the apostle adds, just as Christ glorified God by being the 'Amen' of all His Father's promises, so, when Christians sound the 'Amen', they do so *unto the glory of God*.

21, 22. Paul has played effectively upon the similarity of the meaning of the words 'Yes' and 'Amen'. He now plays upon the affinity of the word 'Amen' with the Hebrew verb meaning to *stablish* or confirm. Those who are concerned with the stupendous affirmation of the gospel, whether they be those who preach it or who respond to the preaching of it (*us with you*) need to be themselves firm and sure in their loyalty to Christ, without any trace of fickleness; and this is precisely what God enables them to be. He 'anoints' all believers, consecrating them to the service of Christ. He 'sets his seal' upon them, marking them out from the rest of mankind as those who really belong to Him and are eternally the objects of His loving care. And He gives them 'in their hearts', i.e. in the innermost recesses of their being, His Spirit as an *earnest* of

48

further and greater blessings to come. The word *arrabōn* translated *earnest* (RSV 'guarantee') was used to describe the portion of purchase money paid on the receipt of goods as a guarantee that the rest of the sum owing would eventually be forthcoming. It was also used of an engagement ring which was a guarantee that the marriage would take place. Paul uses it again in v. 5 of the Spirit who guarantees the immortality of the Christians, and also in Eph. i. 14 of the Spirit who guarantees that the Christian will one day enjoy a divine inheritance.

Paul's teaching in these two verses sounds the same note of the divine initiative as his categorical statement in v. 18 'all things are of God'. It is God who makes men Christians; it is He who anoints them, seals them, and imparts to them the Holy Spirit; a truth which is given symbolic expression in the sacrament of Christian initiation known as Baptism.

c. Reasons for Paul's change of plans (i. 23–ii. 4)

23. The apostle asserts with great solemnity that it was not caprice, or cowardice, or any selfish consideration which led him to change his plans about visiting Corinth. He had acted solely in the interests of the Corinthians. The translation of AV and RV *upon my soul* implies that he summons God as a witness to the truth of what he is saying. If the equally possible rendering of RSV 'against me' is adopted, the meaning is that he is ready to forfeit his life if he is speaking falsely. To visit the Corinthians when they were still unchastened and rebellious would have meant, in the language used by the apostle in 1 Cor. iv. 21, coming to them 'with a rod', and he wished to spare them that unpleasant experience.

. The AV *I came not as yet*, as well as RV 'I forbare to come', was probably influenced by the supposition of the translators that up to the moment of writing Paul had paid only one visit to Corinth. The words *ouketi ēlthon* could, however, equally well be translated 'I came not any more'; in this case the verse probably implies that there had already been a second visit to Corinth of a distressing nature, and Paul would spare the Corinthians a recurrence of it.

24. But, the apostle hastens to add, when he speaks of 'sparing' the Corinthians, he does not mean that he is a tyrant dictating to them in matters of conscience, and determined that they should be in all things subservient to his will. They share equally with him the liberty of the children of God, a liberty subject only to the control of the Holy Spirit. He is their minister and their friend, not a despotic hierarch. No one in fact *can* believe under the pressure of human compulsion, for the urge to believe comes from the Spirit of God. The apostle is confident that the Corinthians are standing firm in their faith (see RSV). But they cannot be isolated believers; they need to be helped to live that disciplined corporate life, whose characteristics are love, joy and peace. Paul's desire, and his duty, is to co-operate with them in promoting the conditions which would enable them to enjoy these blessings. 'We work with you', he says, 'for your joy' (RSV).

ii. 1. We should probably, with RSV, accept the reading 'for' rather than *But*, as it gives a better connection with what precedes. The sense of the verse could be that Paul was determined *either* that his second visit, which had not yet taken place, should not be a sorrowful one; *or* that he would not pay the Corinthians a second sorrowful visit, the implication being that two visits had already been made, the second of which, unrecorded in Acts, was of a painful character. The latter interpretation, made explicit in RSV, is probably right, as in the majority of ancient Greek MSS *again* is found adjacent to *in heaviness* (RV 'with sorrow').

2. Paul has already stated that his dominant wish is to work with the Corinthians to promote their joy. To cause them pain by visiting them may indeed, under exceptional circumstances, be his duty, but he is human enough to be reluctant to discharge it. He longs to share the joy of the Corinthians, to be happy in their happiness; and how can he expect people whom he has saddened to make him cheerful! *Who* is best interpreted in a general sense. No particular individual seems to be in the apostle's mind.

3. The letter mentioned in this verse was taken by older commentators to be the canonical First Epistle to the Corinthians; but it is far more probable that we have here a reference to another letter that has not survived, in which the point made by the apostle in verse 2 was elaborated. *This same* (RV 'this very thing') may indeed mean, as Menzies translates, 'what I have just said'. R. A. Knox has written appositely about the identification of this letter. 'Let a man read 2 Corinthians without any memory of the earlier Epistle, and try to imagine the kind of letter Paul is here referring to—will the picture in his mind be anything like 1 Corinthians? Will he not expect it to be a letter written at white heat on one particular topic, full of complaints and reproaches about that topic predominantly if not exclusively?'[1] In this letter, now lost, Paul had explained why he had not gone straight from Ephesus to Corinth, but had written instead. He had been confident that, when the Corinthians read it, they would understand that by coming to them in their rebellious state he would have experienced only sorrow at the hands of those who knew, *all* of them, in their heart of hearts that they ought to be making him happy and sharing in his happiness.

4. To write that letter had been no easy way out for the apostle. On the contrary, he had not been able to bring himself to the task without much mental anguish and distress; and he was constantly in tears when he wrote it. He knew that his words would hurt; but he denies that his primary object in writing was to wound his readers. He was not trying vindictively to pay off old scores! Rather was he concerned that, painful though the letter had to be, the spirit in which it was written should speak to them of his heart-felt affection. By its position in the Greek the word *love* is given the strongest possible emphasis. All his converts were the objects of Paul's affection; but, as the expression *more abundantly unto you* clearly shows, he had a very special love for the Corinthians. Such

[1] *A New Testament Commentary for English Readers*, Vol. II, p. 179 (Burns, Oates and Washbourne, 1954).

wounds as his words would inflict upon them were, as Moffatt well says, 'the faithful wounds of a friend who had their highest interests at heart in his rebukes':[1] as such they were not far removed from the remedial pains that God in His love allows His wayward children to suffer.

It is surely true that as a description of the apostle's state of mind when he wrote 1 Corinthians his language in this verse, as Plummer points out, would be extravagant.

d. The treatment of the offender (ii. 5-11)

5. The trouble at Corinth that had given rise to the painful letter was caused by a particular offender, for the conditional clause in this verse has a relatival force. The culprit is known but not named; and from this somewhat indirect reference to him it would seem probable that it was Paul himself who had been insulted, either in his absence or on his last visit to Corinth. Older commentators identified the offender with the perpetrator of the incestuous marriage mentioned in 1 Cor. v. 1, assuming that the sentence of excommunication enjoined by Paul had either not been carried out by the Corinthians, or that it had been only temporary, and that the apostle now acquiesced in what they had done. But, as Menzies well says, 'It is quite contrary to the moral position Paul takes up in such questions that he should have tolerated the presence of the incestuous person in the Church, under whatever pressure from his converts, and the person here in question is charged not with immoral but with rude and disagreeable conduct.'

The exegesis of this verse is extremely difficult. AV, taking *you all* as the object of the verb *overcharge*, would seem to be making Paul say that he has suffered only *in part* from the offender's behaviour, for he would not bring a charge of indifference against the Corinthians by suggesting that they had felt no sorrow at what had happened. This interpretation is improbable, for the word *alla*, *but*, does not mean 'except'; and, though Paul had been the offended party, he seems here to

---

[1] *Love in the New Testament*, p. 184 (Hodder and Stoughton, 1929).

be unwilling to regard the offence, even in part, as a personal matter between the offender and himself. RV, and most modern commentators, more naturally construe *you all* as the object of *grieved*; connect *in part* with *you all*; and regard the clause *that I may not overcharge* as parenthetic and explanatory of *in part*. Paul is thus saying that in part all of them have been grieved, but that he adds the words 'in part' so that he 'may not press too heavily'. What he means by this last expression depends upon whether we regard the verb it translates, *epibarō*, as transitive or intransitive. As in other examples of its use it is always transitive, it may be that we ought here to supply 'the offender' as the object. Paul would then be saying that the offence had in fact brought sorrow to every member of the Corinthian church, but that, as he does not want to press too heavily on the offender, he qualifies this statement by adding the words *in part*. As this is a little unnatural, many modern commentators, in spite of the lack of any parallels, treat *epibarō* as intransitive, with the sense 'in order not to keep too great a burden of words', i.e. 'in order not to say too much, and so exaggerate'.[1]

6–8. As the apostle had learned from Titus, the Corinthians, influenced by the painful letter, had taken the essential step of punishing the offender, convinced that the welfare both of the community and of the guilty party necessitated such action. They had not however been unanimous, for a minority had dissented. It would seem that this minority was small, for *tōn pollōn* is more accurately translated by 'the many' (RV) or 'the majority' (RSV) than by *many*. Commentators are not agreed whether it favoured the adoption of less or more severe measures. Paul's tone in the following verses suggests that the latter surmise is the more probable. But, whatever the nature or the degree of the punishment inflicted may have been, the apostle is satisfied that it was adequate. He therefore suggests (for there is nothing in the Greek to justify the insertion of

[1] For a fuller and recent discussion of the word see Arndt and Gingrich, *A Greek-English Lexicon of the New Testament.*

ought) that the Corinthians shall now cease to be penal-administrators, and turn to the opposite and more gracious task of forgiving and comforting the offender. The latter had experienced the grief of penitence; and the apostle sounds the warning that if such sorrow lasts too long or is felt too acutely, it may have a crushing rather than a remedial effect, and perhaps drive the victim into isolation and despair.

Wherefore, he urges in verse 8, both because the man's punishment has been sufficient, and also because there is now a danger of his being overwhelmed by sorrow, the Corinthians would be well-advised to make it transparently clear that their dealings with him from now onwards will be characterized by brotherly love. The translation of *kurōsai* by *confirm* suggests that the apostle is urging them to make their love for the man a matter of certainty. The word could also mean 'decide in favour of love' for him, the assumption being that no decision on the matter had as yet been reached; or 'reaffirm' (so RSV), or 'ratify' by public announcement a decision already reached by them informally (cf. Gal. iii. 15).

9, 10. The letter mentioned in verse 9 is, as in verse 3, the lost letter written between 1 and 2 Corinthians. Paul here implies that the policy of reaffirming love towards the offender, which he has just urged upon the Corinthians, is wholly consistent with the object he had in view when he wrote the painful letter. This is the significance of the word *also*. It is true that in the letter he stressed the need for punishment, and that now he bids them forgive. There is, however, no inconsistency in this, for the letter had not been prompted by a desire for personal vindication that was incompatible with love; it had been written solely that the apostle might test the Corinthians, and discover whether they recognized his authority *in all things*, and not just when it pleased them to do so.

Now that he is satisfied that they have stood the test by agreeing with *his* decision that the offender should be punished, he is prepared, he tells them at the beginning of verse 10, to associate himself whole-heartedly with *their* decision that the penitent should be forgiven.

He forgives the offender, however, not merely as a personal act, but because such forgiveness is necessary for the welfare of the Corinthian church, whose apostle he has been called to be. This is the significance of the words *for your sakes*. And he also forgives *en prosōpō Christou*, which may mean *in the person of Christ*, i.e. 'as Christ's representative' or 'with Christ's authority'. But, as this idea is more usually expressed by *en onomati Christou* (cf. 1 Cor. v. 4), it is more probable that the words mean 'in the presence of Christ' (as RSV).

The clause *if I forgave any thing, to whom I forgave it* is a rather meaningless mistranslation of the reading found in the later MSS. We should follow with RV the reading of the oldest MSS giving the sense 'for what I have forgiven, if I have forgiven anything'. The apostle, in what Plummer calls 'a gracious parenthesis', here states hypothetically what is in reality a fact.

11. Paul now explains further what he meant by *for your sakes* in verse 10. If the offender went unforgiven and was driven to despair after having shown signs of penitence, Satan would *get an advantage* not only over the repentant sinner but over *us*, i.e. the Christian church. 'Some Satan destroys', comments Chrysostom, 'through sin, others through the unmeasured sorrow following on repentance for it . . . conquering us with our own weapons!' No cunning could be more devilish than to turn what is our good into evil. But, as Paul implies, we have been warned about this arch-deceiver, and cannot plead that we are *ignorant of his devices*.

III. PAUL'S APOSTOLIC MINISTRY (ii. 12-vi. 10)

a. Paul's recent journey to Macedonia (ii. 12, 13)

12. Paul now returns to his personal movements after the terrible experience at Ephesus mentioned in i. 8–10. Having abandoned his original plan to journey straight to Corinth for reasons that have been made abundantly plain, Paul went north to Troas. His primary purpose was to preach the gospel in the sea-port town, from which he had previously embarked on his first crossing into Europe (see Acts xvi. 8–11). This evangelistic work would occupy some months, and he naturally supposed that before long he would be joined by Titus on his return from Corinth. Troas provided him with great opportunities. The translation *of the Lord* regards the Greek preposition *en* as instrumental, the door having been opened *by* the Lord. It is better to take it as defining the nature of the opportunity that presented itself to the apostle. It was an opportunity for work in the Lord's service. Hence RV 'in the Lord'.

13. As the weeks passed, without any news of Titus, the apostle could still find no peace of mind.[1] He refers again to this in vii. 5, where the note should be consulted. Eventually he found the suspense intolerable; and, though it meant leaving his work at Troas unfinished, he did not hesitate to press on into Macedonia where Titus would surely meet him at some point on the *Via Ignatia* which spanned the province.

b. Paul's thanksgiving for his share in Christ's triumphs (ii. 14–17)

14. The abandonment of such a promising field of service might have the appearance of weakness. But it was a paramount necessity that the apostle's mind should be set at rest about the state of affairs at Corinth; and we may well believe that failure to obtain reliable information about it was affecting his work. His apostolic ministry, moreover, was not confined to any particular geographical spheres. His 'parish' was the entire Gentile world.

The outburst of thanksgiving that follows was evoked by the memory of his reunion with Titus, not mentioned at this point but spoken of in great detail in chapter vii. Christ's triumphal procession moved steadily forward across the world in spite of apparent set-backs; and in that procession Paul had a

[1] For the force of the Greek tense used here, see J. H. Moulton, *Grammar of New Testament Greek*, Vol. I, p. 145.

proud and honourable place. The meaning of the word *thriambeuō* translated *causeth us to triumph* has been much disputed. RV and RSV, probably rightly, give it its classical meaning 'leads in triumph'. It was used very often in connection with the triumphal processions of emperors and generals, who led in their train the hapless captives they had taken in battle, and exposed them to the gaze of the public. Paul however regards himself as privileged to share in Christ's victory, so that if we adopt the translation 'leads in triumph' we must suppose that the word has lost its original association with military triumphs. AV offers the translation favoured by Augustine and the Latin tradition, but there is no parallel for this use; and, though it is true that Paul would have regarded his own 'victories' as due to God, he seems to be avoiding any reference to himself as a victor. The triumph was Christ's, and wherever Paul is he shares it. He may be led, as R. A. Knox puts it, 'willy-nilly in the conqueror's train', but God uses him *in every place* as the means by which the knowledge of Christ is spread about the world. The gospel of Christ's redeeming love proclaimed by Paul emits a fragrance which penetrates hither and thither like the smoke of incense carried by the wind.

15, 16a. As nothing delights the heart of God more than the preaching of the gospel of Christ, those who proclaim it can truly be described as *a sweet savour unto God*. They are wholly acceptable to Him, though the audiences who listen to them contain those who are on their way to destruction as well as those who are being saved. RV rightly brings out the force of the *present* participles, which is obscured in the translation *them that are saved* and *them that perish*. Paul is not here primarily concerned with the question of predestination. He is simply saying, in Hodge's words, 'The gospel and those who preach it are well-pleasing to God, whether men receive it and are saved, or reject it and are lost.'

In the case of the latter the gospel is, according to the MSS followed by AV, a *savour of death*; it has a deathly smell, and is *unto death*, i.e. results in death, for it is better not to have heard

57

the gospel than having heard it to reject it. RV follows the reading of the more ancient MSS including P.46 which inserts the word 'from' (Gk. *ek*) before the first mention of the words 'death' and 'life'. It is, however, doubtful whether this variant makes any difference to the sense. What Paul is saying is that from start to finish the scent in one case is a deadly fume that must have a killing effect, and in the other its vital fragrance must issue in life. For a similar use of these prepositions cf. the phrase 'from faith unto faith' in Rom. i. 17.

16b, 17. As often before a rhetorical question the conjunction *And* denotes consequence. And so, the apostle implies, in view of the awful results that follow from the preaching of the gospel, who is adequate for such a calling? The particle *for* implies a suppressed answer to this question. That answer could possibly be, 'We apostles are sufficient, as can be seen from the fact that we alone preach an unadulterated gospel.' Vulg. inserts the word 'so' before *sufficient* with the implication 'Who is so sufficient as myself?' But such a note of self-satisfaction would seem ill-fitted to the context. The logic of the passage seems to demand the answer that no one is sufficient for such a high calling in his own unaided strength, for it does not mean carrying the gospel about like a hawker, who adulterates his goods and gives bad measure for the sake of his own personal gain. This is the significance of the colourful word *kapēleuō, corrupt*, which is well brought out by RSV 'pedlars of God's word'. Anyone can preach a whittled-down gospel, in which divine truth is contaminated by the preacher's own views and prejudices, and the notes of severity and urgency are conspicuous by their absence. But only a man who had the sufficiency that is of God can proclaim the full truth as it is in Christ Jesus.

There were many adulterators of the gospel in Paul's day. The Greek expression *hoi polloi* translated *many* is more literally rendered 'the many' by RV, but need not have its full force of 'the majority'. RSV probably rightly gives the meaning 'like so many'. If the variant reading *hoi loipoi*, supported by P.46, is followed the reference would be to 'the others' who were known to the Corinthians. In either case we have evidence here at this early stage in the letter that Paul was conscious that everything was not well at Corinth. This point has an important bearing upon the unity of the Epistle.

Very different from the behaviour of these unscrupulous hucksters is the absolute sincerity that characterized the ministry of Paul. (For the meaning of *eilikrineia, sincerity,* see the note on i. 12.) The apostle's motives were wholly unmixed; he preached as one who had a burden laid upon him by God, who was conscious of the divine presence and enabled others to feel it, and who was so united with Christ, and so imbued with His Spirit, that any tampering with the message committed unto him would have been impossible.

c. Letters testimonial (iii. 1–3)

1. It is not necessary to deduce from this verse, as many modern commentators do, that the charge of self-praise had already been levelled against Paul and that he is here anxious to forestall its repetition. He seems rather to be feeling that, in writing as he has done at the close of the previous chapter, he is giving the impression that the Corinthians know nothing about him, and that he is introducing himself to them *again* and beginning to write a letter of commendation on his own behalf. As a minister of the gospel he has never made use of testimonial letters written by other Christians; and he does not intend to write one in his own interest. He is aware, however, that some teachers have arrived at Corinth bringing letters of this kind from other churches, and expecting to receive similar letters from the Corinthian Christians when they themselves moved elsewhere. We need not infer that Paul regarded all letters of introduction as wrong or unnecessary, though they might sometimes be obtained for malicious purposes, as he himself had once obtained them before his conversion (see Acts ix. 1, 2), and as the false teachers at Corinth had also done. He was probably well aware that the church at Ephesus had written a letter of this kind commending Apollos to the Corinthians (see Acts xviii. 27) and no doubt approved of it. He cannot, however, entertain for a single moment the thought that the Corinthians were so forgetful of his ministry as to need a further testimony to his own credentials.

2, 3. Any additional recommendation of the apostle would in fact have been superfluous, for a fully comprehensive letter of testimony already existed. Paul's converts at Corinth were themselves the living record of the genuineness of his missionary activity. They were in truth his *epistle*, a letter transparently clear to himself, and legible also to others though not written with any material substance such as *ink*. The apostle did not have to be always present with the Corinthians to read this letter; so dear were they to him that in a real sense he carried it about with him wherever he went, and it could be said to be written in his heart. But others could read it as well; in fact, no one, who came into contact with the Christians at Corinth and saw the supernatural change that had been effected in them as a result of their acceptance of the gospel, could fail to read this writing of *the Spirit of the living God*. Such inward, spiritual and divine witness was all the commendation that Paul needed either for the validity of his ministry or for the truth of his gospel.

This writing of the Spirit recalls to the apostle's mind the record of another divine writing which played a momentous part in the story of God's dealings with His people. Moses received from God two tables of stone written with the finger of God containing the precepts of the divine law (Ex. xxxi. 18). Moses was thus in a very real sense a minister of the old covenant. Paul was similarly a minister of the new covenant, for by proclaiming the gospel he enabled the finger of Christ to write an indelible message not on tables of stone but on the *fleshy tables of the heart*. RV, following a better-attested reading, translates 'tables that are hearts of flesh'. This message contained the laws of the new covenant which were in reality not external laws at all, but virtues blossoming into fruit under the influence of the Spirit. Thus was Jeremiah's prophecy fulfilled that God would put His law in men's inward parts and write it in their hearts (see Je. xxxi. 33).

d. The Old and New Covenants (iii. 4–18)

4. The *trust* or confidence that Paul felt in this commendation of his ministry supplied by the Holy Spirit was totally different from the self-confidence of the natural man. It was based neither upon a consciousness of his own innate ability nor upon the good reputation he might have acquired with his fellow-men, but was solely due to the activity of the risen Christ. *Through Christ* alone he possessed it; and he knew in consequence that it would stand the scrutiny of God Himself.

5. What made the apostle so confident about his ministry, in spite of all the difficulties, misunderstandings and trials that it involved, was the certainty that on his own initiative and by the light of his own unaided intellect he could never have devised or comprehended anything so good or so gracious as the gospel. It was God, and God alone, who had revealed His Son in him, who had illuminated his understanding so that he could comprehend the truth as it is in Jesus, and who had sent him forth to proclaim Christ to the Gentiles. By God's grace, and by nothing else, he was what he was (see 1 Cor. xv. 10).

6. The fact that God had chosen men revitalized by His Spirit to be the ministers of the gospel was wholly in keeping with the truth that it was a *new testament* (RV, better, 'covenant') that they were called upon to proclaim. That new covenant, inaugurated by Christ on Calvary, laid upon mankind the obligation not of trying to observe a list of rules and regulations external to themselves, but of accepting the sacrifice of Jesus on the cross as the sole means by which, as sinners, they could be reconciled to God, and of submitting to the guidance of the life-giving Spirit of Christ. A spiritual covenant needs Spirit-filled men as its ministers, for only so can they be *able ministers*.

In the latter half of this verse no contrast is drawn, as has sometimes been supposed, between the outward, verbal form of the Mosaic laws and the spirit underlying them, though it is true that all rules and regulations, whether human or divine, have to be interpreted in the spirit as well as in the letter. Paul is in fact distinguishing the new covenant from the old by using the contrasted categories of spirit and letter, life and death. The Mosaic precepts demanded perfect obedience if life was to be obtained by their means; but since sinners found it impossible to render that obedience, they become liable to the penalty of disobedience, which was nothing less than death (see Rom. vii. 9; Gal. iii. 10). The old covenant, therefore, could not untruly be described as a *letter* which *killeth*. The new covenant, on the other hand, because under it men were endowed with the renewing and invigorating Spirit which removed their sense of impotency, could equally truly be designated as *the spirit* which *giveth life*.

7, 8. But although the Mosaic law 'killed' it had a very necessary function in the education of man's moral sense, for it was, as Paul says in Gal. iii. 24, 'our custodian until Christ came' (RSV). It reflected the character and the purposes of God, and so could be rightly described as *glorious*.

The apostle now allegorizes the account of the giving of the law found in Ex. xxxiv. 29–35, in order to show both the reality and the transience of the glory that was resplendent on that occasion. This account should be read in RV, which gives a more accurate translation of verse 33. When Moses came down from Mount Sinai he was unaware that his skin shone because he had been face to face with God. Aaron and all the children of Israel when confronted with such splendour were afraid to approach him. Moses summoned them to him, and after reciting the commandments to them placed a veil over his face. On returning to the sacred mountain he removed the veil, but when he appeared a second time before the Israelites with his face still resplendent he replaced it. From this story Paul deduced two significant truths: first, that though the law Moses was commanded to promulgate was, as he has already indicated, a *ministration of death*, it was also a revelation of God's glory; and secondly, that the law was not a full or final disclosure either of God's redemptive purposes or of the way in which man would be enabled to glorify his Maker, as he had originally been created to do. The law pointed forward to something intrinsically so superior, viz. *the ministration of the spirit*, that its own glory was destined to be exceeded.

It should be noted that there is nothing in the Exodus narrative corresponding to the participle translated in AV as a prophetic present *which glory was to be done away* (i.e. in Christ), and in RV as a strict imperfect 'which glory was passing away'. The meaning suggested by the AV translation is probably right as will appear in the discussion of verse 13. In any case, Paul infers from the story that the longer Moses remained away from the divine presence, the more the celestial brightness faded from his countenance.

9–11. In these verses the apostle elaborates the contrast which he has already drawn between the two covenants. The greater glory of the new covenant is to be seen, he says, in the superior function it was instituted to discharge. Under the old covenant man was convicted as a sinner and left helpless in his sin; under the new he is put in the right with God, the demands of the law having been satisfied in Him who inaugurated it (verse 9). So great is this qualitative difference between *condemnation* and *righteousness* or acquittal, that the splendour of the old covenant is far outshone by the glory of the new—so much so that by comparison it scarcely appears to be glorious at all (verse 10). Finally, the permanence of the new dispensation, standing out in contrast to the temporary character of the old, gives it an abiding glory. The old, it is true, had its splendour; but, in the words of R. A. Knox, 'its glory is now dimmed like the shine of lamps when dawn comes'.

12. Paul is living under the new covenant. He has experienced its glory and he reflects it in his ministry; but great as that glory is, it has not yet been fully displayed. It remains a *hope*, but the hope is so well-founded that there is nothing hesitant about Paul's preaching. On the contrary, he uses *great plainness* (RV 'boldness') *of speech*. He is, as the word *parrēsia* suggests, both courageous and outspoken. Confident of the reality of God's dealings with him, and certain of his divine mission, he can face his fellow-men without any fear of the consequences.

13. This frankness, so characteristic of Paul's ministry, was not conspicuous in the ministry of Moses. This was not due to any moral failure on the part of Moses. It was inherent in the very nature of the revelation he mediated. He was concerned very largely with types and shadows, in which truth was very often wrapped up in mystery and symbol; and the mystery remained till the archetype was made known and the reality became visible.

Paul illustrates this from the Exodus story, and underlines the secondary inference that he has drawn from it in passing in verse 7. Moses, he says in effect, veiled his face not only because the Israelites shrank back from its brightness, but also because he knew that the glory upon it was fading; and in the providence of God, though not necessarily in the express and conscious design of Moses himself, the Israelites were not to see that the fading was symbolic of the ultimate abolition of the old dispensation. The AV translation *could not stedfastly look to the end of that which is abolished* leaves the reader to infer that the abolition would take place when Christ came, who was Himself *the end* or fulfilment of the old order. In the providence of God the Israelites, under the Mosaic dispensation, were able to enjoy only a revelation that was preparatory to something better. The sacrifices enjoined upon them were temporary and inferior sacrifices, the blood of bulls and goats; those who offered them could not see *the end* to which they were pointing, viz. the perfect sacrifice of Christ, which inaugurated the new covenant, and so had as its corollary the abolition of the old.

This interpretation of what is a very difficult verse is that of most of the ancient fathers. It has the merit of giving a satisfactory meaning to *the end*, indeed the only satisfactory one, if

R. A. Knox is correct in saying that the Greek *to telos* 'denotes everywhere a point not a process, and the notion it regularly conveys is that of fulfilment'.

Most modern commentators take the participle not as a prophetic present but as an imperfect, and adopt the RV rendering 'the end of that which was passing away'. They are moreover unwilling to tie the meaning down so definitely as the AV, and tend to assume that Paul, accused of 'veiling his gospel', defends himself by recalling somewhat whimsically this incident in the Old Testament in which 'a veiling' played a conspicuous part. All that he is in effect supposed to be saying is, 'whatever may have happened then, there is nothing veiled about *my* gospel'.

14, 15. The apostle has already implied that it was part of the divine dispensation that the ancient Israelites should not see the temporary character of the old dispensation. God had in fact dulled their understanding. *Their minds were blinded* means in effect that God had blinded them (cf. Rom. xi. 7; Jn. xii. 40). RV substitutes 'hardened' for *blinded*, probably wrongly, for the noun *pōrōsis*, cognate with the verb used here, denotes obtuseness or intellectual blindness.[1] The same obtuseness was to be found unchanged among the numerous Jews of Paul's own day who refused to see that Jesus as the Christ was the fulfilment of the old law, and who, in consequence, rejected Paul's gospel. There was, then, a sense in which it was true to say that the veil, seen by the Israelites on Moses' face, was still covering the minds of the Jewish people when they heard the books of the old covenant read in their synagogues. It was still *untaken away* (RV 'unlifted'). AV and RV understand the Greek at the beginning of the last clause of verse 14 as the relative *ho ti*, and translate *which vail*. Most other editions, however, assume it to be the causal *hoti*, and usually understand the sentence to mean 'the veil remains unlifted, because it is removed only in Christ' (see RSV). The general sense is in

[1] See the full discussion of these words in J. A. Robinson, *Epistle to the Ephesians*, pp. 264–274.

either case the same. The rejection of the Christ by the Jews of necessity implies that the veil is still obscuring their spiritual vision. Few passages in the New Testament emphasize more strongly than this that the Old Testament Scriptures are only fully intelligible when Christ is seen to be their fulfilment.

16. Once more the apostle's language is coloured by the Exodus narrative, especially by Ex. xxxiv. 35. When (or as the Greek means 'whenever') Moses went in before the Lord, he removed the veil. The direct vision of God that he was in this way privileged to enjoy was denied to the Israelites to whom he had been speaking. They had to be content with a more partial knowledge of God conveyed to them through the medium of the law. And so whenever Moses turned to the Lord, he could by inference be also said to have turned away from the law that he had been promulgating. Similarly, Paul argues, whenever a Jew *shall turn to the Lord*, the Lord being the Christ, and sees in Him the fulfilment of the Mosaic law, the veil has been clearly dropped. For whenever any man or woman turns to Christ and confronts Him in direct personal encounter, it is a sign that everything that has hitherto interposed itself between the believer and his Saviour has now been removed.

17. The apostle now explains why 'turning to the Lord' involves the removal of the veil spread over men's hearts. It is because *the Lord* mentioned in the previous verse, who has already been interpreted as the Christ in whom the Old Testament is fulfilled, is also one with the Holy Spirit. Paul is not here confounding the Persons of the Trinity by identifying Christ and the Spirit, but showing that because of the Holy Spirit the influence of Christ is universal in its effect and unlimited in its power. The Lord and the Spirit are 'one' in the same sense that Jesus said that He and the Father were one (Jn. x. 30). Christ transforms the inner lives of men because the Spirit takes of what is His and reveals it to them (see Jn. xvi. 14). The influence of Christ and the influence of the Holy Spirit cannot, therefore, be distinguished.

The translators of AV inserted the word *that*, which is not found in the original, apparently because they thought there is here a reference back to verse 6. In that verse they understood Paul to be saying that it was the Spirit that gave life to the Mosaic regulations, and they assumed accordingly that in this verse he was making it clear that *that* Spirit was in fact the Lord, i.e. Christ. It is, however, of the present influence of Christ that this verse is speaking, and RV rightly omits *that*. As Menzies pertinently comments, 'Christ is not a man who has died and is present to the Church mainly by his words which are remembered, but a divinity, capable of being in every place at once, and of inspiring all hearts.'

The Holy Spirit is Christ's Spirit, and *where the Spirit of the Lord* is there is freedom from every kind of bondage, whether to the law (Gal. v. 18), or to fear (Rom. viii. 15), or to sin (Rom. vii. 6), or to corruption (Rom. viii. 21, 23). Even a converted slave could rejoice in the glorious liberty of a child of God.

18. In this closing verse of the section Paul speaks of the transformation that is being daily effected in the lives of those who have no veil coming between them and the Lord, and who are indwelt by the Holy Spirit. *With open* (RV 'unveiled') *face* the Christian has a real vision of *the glory of the Lord*, but, if the AV translation is right, it is only *as in a glass* or mirror that he can now see it. As ancient mirrors were made of metal and had a dull reflecting surface, the vision must of necessity be imperfect. What the Christian sees is, in Hodge's words, 'not the immediate, beatific vision of the glory of the Lord, which is only enjoyed in heaven, but that manifestation of his glory which is made in his word and by his Spirit, whose office it is to glorify Christ by revealing him to us.' This may well be the right interpretation. It involves understanding the Greek word *katoptrizō*, which in the middle voice generally has the meaning 'beholding oneself in a mirror', as having in this passage the active sense of 'beholding something else as in a mirror', and for this the authority of Philo can be quoted.

There does not seem to be any evidence except that of Chrysostom to justify the RV rendering 'reflecting as a mirror', though this is favoured by most modern commentators on the ground that it suits the context. Moses could not reflect the glory he himself had seen but had to veil his face; but the Christian, somewhat like the mirror of a modern heliograph, can transmit to others directly such glory as he has himself been able to see. Chrysostom seems to regard the word as having the double meaning of beholding and reflecting, and he comments: 'Just as if pure silver be turned towards the sun's rays, it will itself also shoot forth rays, not from its own natural property merely, but also from the solar lustre; so doth the soul being cleansed, and made brighter than silver, receive a ray from the glory of the Spirit, and glance it back.' It would, however, seem more natural to suppose that it is by *beholding* the image of Christ, rather than by reflecting it, that the Christian becomes changed into it. No doubt it is true that what he sees is reflected by him to others, but we cannot be sure that this is what is being said in this verse.

The makers of RSV seem to regard the metaphor of the mirror as no longer alive in the word, and they translate by 'beholding' in the text and 'reflecting' in the margin. But, whatever may be the exact significance of this difficult word, the main emphasis in the verse is upon the transformation in the Christian as he contemplates the glory of God on the face of Jesus Christ.

The expression *from glory to glory* may mean that the glory seen in Christ creates a similar glory in the Christian; or that the Christian advances from one stage of glory to another. In either case what makes the transformation possible is *the Spirit of the Lord*. This translation is favoured by Vulg. *a domini spiritu*; but, as in the Greek 'Lord' precedes 'Spirit', it is not the most natural rendering. Modern scholars, therefore, rightly retain the original order and construe the two words in apposition. So RV 'the Lord the Spirit', and RSV 'the Lord who is the Spirit'. This brings the thought into line with what has been said in verse 17, and interprets the words as the similar expression in Gal. i. 3 must be interpreted, 'God who is our Father'.

Those who translate the parallel words found in verse 17 as 'the Spirit is the Lord' do not hesitate to make a similar inversion here; but though such a transposition was favoured by the early Greek Fathers, it would seem that they were unduly influenced by the desire to find additional scriptural authority for the divinity of the Holy Spirit.

e. The 'openness' of the apostolic ministry (iv. 1-6)

1. It is such a ministry as *this* that has been entrusted to Paul, a ministry of the new covenant, superior to that of Moses, and through it the glory of God can shine unveiled. It has moreover been committed to him by the unmerited *mercy* of God. Therefore he does not *faint*; he does not shrink from the duties it lays upon him, but discharges them with frankness, alacrity and courage.

2. The use of the English perfect *have renounced* to translate the aorist tense of the original is correct, because Paul is not drawing attention to any particular moment in the past when he made this renunciation, but is rather describing some general characteristics of his ministry. As Plummer points out, the translation *the hidden things of dishonesty* was accurate in 1611, when 'dishonesty' and 'disgrace' were synonyms. This meaning is now archaic, and RV falls back upon the literal but not very lucid rendering 'the hidden things of shame'. RSV 'disgraceful underhanded ways' is preferable. Paul's methods, he insists, are always open and above-board. Not for him the subtleties of the unscrupulous politician or the subterfuges of the ingratiating salesman! He does not *walk in craftiness* (the same word *panourgia* being used as is found in xi. 3 to describe the manner in which Satan beguiled Eve). Nor does he *handle the word of God deceitfully*. He does not, for example, dilute its severity to make himself popular with his hearers; nor does he confound it with human philosophies, but proclaims it for what in fact it is, *the* (revealed) *truth*. And the preacher who presents such truth directly and faithfully commends it *to every man's conscience*, for while the intellects of men and women may be attracted by the sophistries and subtleties of 'the essayist in the pulpit', it is the plain unadulterated gospel of the grace of God revealed supremely in the death and resurrection of Christ that alone strikes home to his *conscience*. 'Repent and believe the gospel' must ever be the burden of one who is preaching *in the sight of God*.

3, 4. But Paul well knew that many who hear the gospel remain unbelievers. They may hear it with their ears, but it is not accepted as having any relevance for themselves, and so *is hid* as far as they are concerned. Paul is here stating in different language the teaching of Jesus in the parable of the sower. He is not implying that everyone who does not accept the gospel on any particular occasion is of necessity permanently *lost*, though, in some cases, this may be so. The Greek participle is more correctly translated 'are perishing' as in RV and RSV. As long as men are on the road to perdition the gospel is veiled to them; and they are in this situation because of the activity of *the god of this world*. The teaching of the New Testament would seem to be that Satan and his satellites are by no means yet overcome, though their death-knell was sounded by Christ's victory on the cross. These sinister forces are, in fact, so powerful that Jesus described their leader as 'the *prince* of this world', and Paul here designates him 'the *god* of this world'. Unbelief and blindness of spiritual vision caused by this evil potentate are closely related, and it is impossible to state definitely which is cause and which is effect. But, when they are present, there is a darkness that *the light of the . . . gospel of Christ* cannot penetrate. AV takes 'the glory' as a qualifying genitive signifying *the glorious gospel*. It is more meaningful to take it as an objective genitive in the sense that the gospel reveals the glory of Christ; it enables men to see His essential splendour. This glory was present in His earthly life, but only after suffering and death did He enter fully into His glory (see Lk. xxiv. 26). It was Christ in *glory* who appeared to Paul on the Damascus road and, in consequence, the gospel was to him primarily 'the gospel of the glory of Christ' (RV). Unlike the original twelve apostles he had not begun by knowing Jesus in His incarnate life; he was able, therefore, to grasp more quickly than they the truth that Christ was *the image of God*, in whom the likeness of God was fully present, so that all who have seen Him have seen the Father (see Jn. xii. 45, xiv. 9).

5. Paul now underlines the truth that what he preaches is the gospel of Christ. Any other so-called 'gospel' would be no gospel at all, but only an exhibition of the speaker's own opinions, prejudices and idiosyncrasies. The business of a preacher is to draw attention not to himself, but to Christ; to proclaim the crucified and risen Jesus as the Messiah in whom God's purposes, expressed in the Old Testament, are fulfilled; as the Saviour who liberates men from the guilt and power of sin; and as *the Lord* who demands the total allegiance and obedience of the believer. All the service Paul (and every true Christian missionary and pastor) renders to his converts is not done *primarily* for their sakes. He has a more compelling love and a more overriding loyalty. He is their servant, because first and foremost he is the servant of Jesus Christ, by whose love he is constrained, and the promotion of whose glory is his passionate desire.

6. The connecting particle *For* seems to give the reason first, why Paul preaches Jesus, and secondly, why he is the servant of the Corinthians. His own heart has been divinely illumined, not only that he himself may be able to see who Jesus really is, but also that he may bring the knowledge of what he has seen to others. 'In the light which flashed into his heart, he saw the face of Jesus Christ, and knew that the glory which shone there was the glory of God' (Denney). But what he had himself first seen and heard on the Damascus road could not remain a selfish possession. 'It was the good pleasure of God', he told the Galatians, 'who separated me, even from my mother's womb . . . to reveal his Son in me, that I might

71

preach him among the Gentiles' (Gal. i. 15, 16, RV; cf. Acts xxvi. 15, 16).

Conversion was to Paul a miraculous new birth, a constantly recurring display of God's creative and redemptive power. The only adequate parallel to the penetration of the darkness of the sinful human heart by the kindly light of God's grace was the dispersal of the darkness that originally covered the face of the deep by the divine fiat 'Let there be light' (Gn. i. 3). But there is a sense in which even greater splendour can be said to accompany the new creation than the old. For, as Chrysostom comments, 'Then indeed He said, Let it be and it was: but now He said nothing, but Himself became light for us. For the apostle does not say, "has also now commanded" but "has Himself shined".'

f. The contrast between the message and the messenger (iv. 7–15)

7. To know *the glory of God in the face of Jesus Christ* and to be called to spread this knowledge is the most treasured of all possessions. But the wonder of the divine dispensation is that while an earthly treasure is usually preserved in a container of fitting dignity and beauty, the treasure of the gospel has been entrusted to men subject to the infirmities and limitations, the instability and insecurity of their finite condition. It is as though a most costly jewel were encased in an earthenware jar! Paul sees in this a supreme manifestation of the divine law that God's strength is made perfect in human weakness (cf. xii. 9). This striking paradox makes it clear that the gospel is no product of human ingenuity, no clever discovery of the human intellect, no bright idea of some outstanding genius, but a revelation of the power of the sovereign God. He may choose learned or unlearned men to be ministers of this gospel, but though 'chosen vessels' (see Acts ix. 15) they are all *earthen* vessels, in which 'another's jewel is kept, lamps of clay in which another's light shines' (Denney).

8, 9. In a series of four pairs of participles Paul now contrasts the humiliating circumstances in which he often finds himself

as a minister of the gospel, with the divine power which re-
deems them and makes them occasions for further manifesta-
tions of God's glory. Never, it seems, are his enemies allowed to
do their worst. *Troubled . . . yet not distressed* fails to bring out
the underlying metaphor, which seems to be that of a com-
batant who gives his opponent little room for action, but is
nevertheless unable to drive him into a corner where no
movement is possible. The apostle is 'hemmed in on every
side', but not completely restricted. In the second of the series
emphasis is laid on the limited means that, humanly speaking,
are available for Paul. He is without proper provision, but not
totally so. The play here on the Greek words *aporoumenoi* and
exaporoumenoi might be kept by some such rendering as 'at a
loss but not at a loss that matters' (cf. Denney's suggestion
'put to it, but not utterly put out'). For *persecuted* RV has
'pursued'. This retains the suggestion in the original that Paul
is a hunted man, who is nevertheless *not forsaken*, i.e. not
abandoned to the enemy, nor left solely to his own resources.
Persecuted in one city, he often has to escape to another (see
Mt. x. 23), but only to find fresh opportunities for Christian
witness. Finally, even when he was hunted down, and it
seemed as if he had been smitten to the ground never to rise
again (as at Lystra, Acts xiv. 19), he was not *destroyed*, but
stood on his feet once more and continued his ministry.

10. The apostle's life, he submits, could not untruly be
regarded as a reflection of the *dying* life that Jesus Himself was
compelled to experience, and was glad to experience, in the
discharge of His vocation as the Redeemer of the world. The
fourfold mention of the name *Jesus* in this verse and the following is most significant, for it shows how constantly the story of
the earthly life of the Saviour was in his mind. He is *bearing
about in the body* not the death, but *the dying (nekrōsis*; Vulg.
mortificatio) of Jesus. (The best MSS omit *the Lord*.) As Paul well
knew, Jesus had to spend much physical strength and spiritual
energy in the service of others; He was relentlessly hunted
down by his political and religious opponents; He experienced

sleepless nights and exhausting days with nowhere to lay His head. It might indeed be said that the death that He ultimately died was but the final stage of a *dying* that had been continuous while He trod the way of obedience as the Suffering Servant of God. Paul can indeed understand with a sympathy born of similar experiences this dying life that Jesus lived on earth. But as 'a man in Christ' he can also enjoy the power of his Master's resurrection. His own frequent and remarkable escapes from death were in fact irrefutable signs that the power of the risen Jesus was being revealed here and now in his own body. The apostles were thus witnesses in deed as well as in word to the truth of their Lord's resurrection.

11. *Bearing about in the body the dying of Jesus* is, however, something more than the language of mysticism. It is strictly true to the facts. During the whole of his life as a minister of the gospel Paul was daily experiencing something of the feelings that come to men under sentence of death. Never could he be sure that he would be alive on the morrow. To live *for Jesus' sake* involved the readiness to suffer physically and mentally for His sake; it meant being hated for His sake; and it carried with it the liability of being put to death for His sake (see 1 Cor. iv. 9 and xv. 30). But the fact that the suffering did not overwhelm him, that the world's hatred did not overcome him, and that the martyrdom that seemed always so inevitable and so imminent had so far been postponed, was in itself evidence that a supernatural power, *the life of Jesus*, was being *made manifest* in his *mortal flesh*.

12. We should probably not follow Calvin in interpreting this verse ironically, as though Paul were saying in effect, 'You see that I have all the suffering and you reap the benefits'. Rather would the apostle appear to be saying in all seriousness that, because his sufferings afford evidence of the risen power of Jesus, they are a source of life, to those to whom he ministers, the life that can be found in Jesus alone.

13. But, even if the wonderful benefits brought by his sufferings to his converts were not apparent, Paul would not lose heart under the burdens imposed upon him. Still less would he abandon the ministry of the word. He would continue to give expression to the faith that is in him. For this, he affirms, is the vocation of every true believer, and not merely of those especially called to be evangelists. All true servants of God, such as the writer of Psalm cxvi, whose words Paul here quotes, are compelled by their faith, even at times when 'the sorrows of death compass them and the pains of hell gat hold upon them', to give spontaneous expression to their belief, to call upon their Lord, and to express their confidence in His goodness. This is both a sign of the reality of their faith and an inevitable product of it. Paul shares this *spirit of faith* with the Psalmist. He cannot envisage the possibility of an inarticulate believer. As Denney well comments, 'Not all the believing are to be teachers and preachers, but all are to be confessors. Everyone who has faith has a witness to bear to God.'

14. The author of Psalm cxvi was saved from acute danger. Paul too has again and again been rescued from what seemed to be the jaws of death. One day, however, death will lay his icy hand upon him, as it does upon all mankind, even upon the greatest of God's saints; and this may happen before his Lord returns in glory. But he remains undaunted by the prospect, for it is an essential element of his faith that the power of God, shown in the resurrection of Jesus from the dead, will be manifested again in himself and in all believers. 'God', he asserts, 'will raise us also with Jesus and bring us with you into his presence' (RSV). The best MSS read 'with Jesus' not *by Jesus*, and the preposition means 'in virtue of our union with Jesus'. All who are 'in Christ' *remain* 'in Christ', whether they be alive or dead. *His* resurrection is the pledge of *their* resurrection. Because He lives, they will live also. The communion of saints cannot be destroyed by death. They are for ever with their Lord.

15. Because all who are 'in Christ' are united with one another, Paul cannot contemplate his own future blessedness apart from that of his converts, any more than he has been able to think of his own personal sufferings without remembering the benefits they have brought to others. All his experience has as its ultimate object the eternal welfare of his converts. *All things*, he cries, *are for your sakes* and, ultimately, for God's sake, for the more people who come to know the grace of God through the gospel Paul preaches, the more numerous will be the thanksgivings that will be evoked, and the greater the praise that will be offered to God. In a word, that God may be increasingly glorified, not that he himself may be exalted, is Paul's supreme ambition.

g. **Outward decline and inward renewal** (iv. 16-18)

16. In view of the divine power which has so often aided him and with the prospect of a glorious resurrection ever before him, the apostle does not 'lose heart' (RSV). He does not *faint* through weariness of spirit, but continues to give his Christian witness with courage and determination. Nevertheless, his sufferings, though they have not yet proved fatal, are inevitably exhausting his physical strength. His *outward man*, a unique and comprehensive expression including all that is implied in *earthen vessel* (verse 7), *our body* (verse 10), and *mortal flesh* (verse 11), 'is decaying' (RV). But at the same time his *inward man* (RSV 'inner nature') *is renewed day by day*. Though it is impossible to define exactly the expression 'inward man', it would seem, as Plummer suggests, to refer to 'the highest part of our immaterial being, which is capable of being the home of the Holy Spirit and of being ruled by Him'. This daily renewal is the vast compensation which only a Christian can experience. As his earthly faculties fade the things of the Spirit become more real to him. Denney well comments: 'The decay of the outward man in the godless is a melancholy spectacle, for it is the decay of everything; in the Christian it does not touch the life which is hid with Christ in God, and which is in the soul itself a well of water springing up to life eternal.'

17. Because of this daily renewal, the glory of heaven seems to transfigure the apostle's afflictions and to make them appear comparatively light and of brief duration. Viewed from any other standpoint his sufferings would seem exceedingly grievous and far from temporary; for, as Hodge remarks, 'It was only by bringing these sufferings into comparison with eternal glory that they dwindled into insignificance'. The apostle's own experiences in the service of his Master confirmed the truth of the Saviour's words that the inheritance of eternal life was a direct consequence of suffering endured for His sake (see Mt. xix. 29). We must suffer with Christ, Paul says in Rom. viii. 17, that we may be glorified with Him. 'If we endure', he tells Timothy, 'we shall reign with him' (2 Tim. ii. 12, RV). It is not that present affliction for Christ's sake merits future glory; but it does nevertheless procure it, and it does so 'more and more exceedingly' (so RV taking the expression *kath huperbolēn eis huperbolēn* with the verb, and not with *weight of glory* as AV).

18. The participial expression at the beginning of this verse is taken in a temporal sense in AV and RV *while we look*. RSV interprets it causally 'because we look'; and some commentators construe it conditionally 'if we look'. Perhaps the sense is best conveyed by 'looking as we do'. During the period that must elapse before Paul can experience the glory that awaits him, he turns his gaze more and more away from *the things which are seen*, i.e. the troubles that are his present lot, to *the things which are not seen*, i.e. 'the things which God hath prepared for them that love him' (1 Cor. ii. 9). This is the goal that he keeps steadily in view; and he does so because these visible things are *temporal* (RSV 'transient'). The afflictions will pass, and the night of sorrow will end. On the other hand, the invisible things, the joy of his Lord into which one day he will enter, the inheritance for him in heaven, are eternal.

h. The Christian hope (v. 1–10)

1. Paul now gives a further reason why he is undismayed by the growing consciousness of his failing faculties and the increasing awareness that his sufferings will ultimately result in his death. His human body, as he is becoming more and more conscious, is a temporary structure, adequate to shelter him during the few brief years of his earthly pilgrimage, but as vulnerable to the winds of circumstance and the wear and tear of everyday life as a *tabernacle* or tent. This *earthly house* will most surely be *dissolved* in death, unless he survives till the Lord's return; in which case his present body will be transformed into the spiritual, or resurrection, body. The latter possibility seems to him remote; yet the prospect of the inevitable alternative does not fill him with alarm or despondency. On the contrary, it is a joyful expectation, for he is convinced (*we know*) that the shelter that awaits him after death is as superior to that provided by the present body as the protection of a solid well-built house is superior to that of a tent. That better shelter already exists. *We have it*, he writes, *in the heavens*. Its sole architect is God; no human hands have constructed it, or play any part in its maintenance. It is *a building of God, an house not made with hands*, and it has been fashioned to last for ever. It was this *eternal* shelter, described as 'mansions' or dwelling-places, that Jesus told His disciples He was going on ahead to make ready for them (see Jn. xiv. 2).

2. In a not uncharacteristic manner Paul now changes the metaphor, though his thought remains the same. The shelter that awaits the Christian after death is pictured as a garment which can be put on over another garment. Hence the expression *clothed upon with*. This has led many modern commentators to conclude that, throughout this passage, it is the resurrection body which is being portrayed, first as a heavenly house and secondly as a heavenly garment. On this interpretation Paul is supposed to be saying either that in this present body (*in this* looking back to *tabernacle*) he groans and earnestly desires to be *clothed upon with* the *house which is from heaven*, i.e. his resurrection body; or that the subject of his groaning (*in this* pointing forward to the participle) is his earnest desire to obtain this blessing. Moreover, if the double compound in the verb *ependusasthai*, translated *clothed upon with*, is stressed, the

inference can be drawn that Paul longed to have this resurrection body put on over his present body as an additional
vesture. In other words, he wanted to be alive when the Lord
returned, so that his earthly body could be changed into a
spiritual body without the dissolution of death. Paul, however,
often changes his metaphors; nor does he consistently distinguish simple verbs from compounds; and, as there is no clear
reference to the Lord's return in the passage, it may well be
that the sense of the verse is that the sufferings of the apostle
are accompanied by groanings because he longs for the more
permanent, heavenly (the meaning of *from heaven*) shelter
which awaits him after death.

3. There are two main problems in this very difficult verse.
First, at the beginning of the sentence, some Greek MSS read
ei per and others *ei ge*; the former usually allows for some
uncertainty and has the significance of 'provided that', while
the latter suggests that there is really no doubt at all and
conveys the suggestion 'if as we have every right to assume'.
It is probable however that the distinction is not always
observed in the Greek of the New Testament. AV and RV
translate *if so be that*, and RSV 'so that'.

Secondly, the words *being clothed* could be taken either as in
agreement with the subject of the verb, or as its predicate in
conjunction with *not . . . naked*. The English versions, rightly it
would seem, take them in the former manner; in this case the
probable sense is 'assured that when we have put on this
clothing (i.e. obtained this more substantial shelter) we shall
not be found to be naked (i.e. without house or home)'. Those
who take *being clothed* as the predicate usually construe it as a
passive with the sense 'found to be *already* clothed'. But, as the
participle in all the Greek MSS is in the middle voice, there
would seem to be no justification for this line of interpretation.
Those who indulge in it vary in the deductions they draw. If
they assume that the situation envisaged in the passage is the
day of the Lord's return, they regard Paul as saying in effect
'assured that we shall then be found still possessing our earthly

body and not naked spirits'; the inference being that there will be no interval, when the soul will be in a disembodied state, having lost its earthly body without having received its body from heaven. On the other hand, those who imagine that the situation envisaged is the day of Paul's death, believe that Paul is sounding a *caveat* about the assurance stated in the previous verse. The blessedness that awaits the Christian after death is subject, he would be saying, to the condition that on that day the soul is found to be clothed with the necessary qualifications and not caught unprepared. Calvin's interpretation, for example, is that men must be found clothed with the righteousness of Christ before they can pass on after death to the shelter of heaven. Similarly, Catholic expositors, following the passive participle of the Vulgate *vestiti*, assume the meaning to be that the soul must be found in a state of grace, if it is finally to enter into glory.[1]

It would seem that the following four considerations should be determinative for the interpretation of this verse: (i) it is more probable that Paul is substantiating rather than qualifying what he has just said; (ii) we are not justified in taking the participle *clothed upon* as a passive predicate; (iii) the context suggests that Paul has in mind the probability of his death rather than the possibility of his being alive when the Lord returns; (iv) it is unlikely that he is contradicting what he has said in 1 Corinthians xv by suggesting that the resurrection body may be bestowed on him immediately after death.

We conclude, then, that the probability is that Paul is here underlining his certainty that a heavenly shelter awaits him immediately after death, and making it clear that that certainty is in no way diminished by the thought that his departure to be with Christ may precede the Lord's return in glory and his own assumption of the resurrection body.

[1] R. A. Knox translates 'if death, when it comes, finds us sheltered and not defenceless against the winds': cf. his exegesis of the passage in *A New Testament Commentary for English Readers*, Vol. II, p. 186 (Burns, Oates and Washbourne, 1954).

4. The apostle's intense desire to be *clothed upon*, i.e. to enjoy the protection of an imperishable heavenly shelter, is not prompted by a fanatic's desire to be rid of his body at all costs because of its frailty and manifold frustrations, nor, it would seem, by the more worthy hope that he might be alive to receive his resurrection body from the hands of his returning Lord, and so be spared the experience of death altogether. He does not want to be unclothed at all; but he is very sure that if his earthly body should be dissolved in death, a blessed home beyond the grave awaits him. The almost intolerable burden of sorrow and suffering laid upon him during his life *in this tabernacle* (RSV 'in this tent') leads him indeed to *groan* (he would be less than human if it did not); but the groaning is also prompted by the desire to be more abundantly and better *clothed* when he passes after death into an existence, where all that is mortal in him will have ceased to be and he himself will be absorbed into the fuller life of heaven.

5. The apostle now insists that nothing he has just said is the product of wishful thinking. The truth is that God has re-created the Christians in order that He may, in the words of the Epistle to the Hebrews, bring many sons to glory. All His dealings with those who are 'in Christ' have this as their ultimate object; and He has both made them aware of His purposes and given them the assurance that a blessed life awaits them after death by the presence within them of His Holy Spirit. The Spirit Himself creates the longings of which Paul gives expression; He is the ultimate author of the groanings that fall from time to time from the believers' lips; and He is *the earnest* (RSV 'guarantee') of their immortality. (For the significance of the word *arrabōn*, *earnest*, see note on i. 22.)

6–8. The presence of the Holy Spirit, Paul here asserts, is the source not only of his unshakable confidence as he looks out on the future, but also of his sustained courage as he faces the present. The word translated *confident*, *tharrountes*, is more accurately rendered 'of good courage', as in RV. This courage never fails the Christian, however great the dangers that confront him. It is *always* possible for him to show it, because the Holy Spirit is always present with him. Despair is therefore an experience to which he does not submit; for to despair is to disown the Spirit, and to disown the Spirit is not to be a Christian at all. Particularly does this courage come to the Christian's aid when he contemplates his death. The natural sense of loss at leaving the body that has been his earthly home is overlaid by the certainty that the best is yet to be. He knows that, though he is already 'in Christ' and lives in union with Him as a member of His body, yet he is not yet *with* Christ, and so can be said to be *absent from the Lord*. He lives *by faith*; he does not see his Redeemer as He is in the fulness of His glory, and is not conscious of His *abiding* presence.

The parenthetical words in verse 7 may imply that the controlling force of the believer's life is not the invisible heavenly things, but faith that these things exist. In that case *sight, eidos*, would have a passive significance. On the other hand, if *eidos* has a more active sense, the apostle is saying that the determining factor is faith in Christ even though the believer cannot yet see Him face to face.

9, 10. But it is not only confidence and courage that the Christian needs in the face of death. Death not only enables him to be with Christ; it also brings him nearer the day when, in company with the rest of mankind, he will have to submit to the scrutiny of divine judgment. Then the secrets of all hearts will be disclosed; and because much is required of those to whom much has been given, the thought of the judgment seat of Christ has for the Christian a peculiar solemnity. It is not meant to cloud his prospect of future blessedness, but to act as a stimulus, as strong a stimulus as the most imperious of human ambitions; for the word *philotimoumetha*, translated *we labour* (RV 'we make it our aim'), means literally 'we are ambitious'. It should spur him on to scale the heights of Christian living, and to be always, whether *present or absent* (i.e. come life, come death), well-pleasing unto his Lord.

Some commentators stress the seeming inconsistency between the doctrine of justification by faith alone and the doctrine of verse 10 that Christians, no less than non-Christians, will be finally judged by their actions. This stressing of seemingly opposite emphases is, however, of special value to the Christian and prevents him from underestimating his moral obligations. As Denney well comments: 'It is not necessary for us to seek a formal reconciliation of this verse with Paul's teaching that the faithful are accepted in Christ Jesus; we can feel that both must be true. And if the doctrine of justification freely by God's grace is that which has to be preached to sinful men, the doctrine of exact retribution, taught in this passage, has its main interest and importance for Christians.'

i. The constraining love of Christ (v. 11–15)

11. The thought of divine judgment engenders in the apostle a permanent feeling of awe and reverence. This is expressed better in the RV 'the fear of the Lord', where the genitive is taken objectively in the sense of reverence for the Lord, than in the AV *the terror of the Lord*, where the genitive is regarded as subjective in the sense of the terror which the Lord inspires. Paul's primary work is to *persuade men* of the truth of the gospel (see Acts xviii. 4 and xxviii. 23); and had he not continually 'walked in the fear of the Lord' (see Acts ix. 31), he might have yielded to the temptation to curry favour with his hearers by whittling down his message to suit their tastes. But the knowledge that his inmost motives were fully known to God, to whom alone he was responsible, and that they would stand the test of His scrutiny, acted as a brake upon the natural desire to please others, freed him from paralysing inhibitions, and removed the undue sensitiveness he might otherwise have felt when subjected to the unjust criticism of his fellows. He confidently trusts that, however much others may defame him, the Corinthians, with whom he has had such personal and intimate associations, will have become convinced by now of his integrity—every one of them, as the plural *consciences* seems to imply.

12. The apostle has certainly not been disclosing some of his deepest religious feelings merely to try and convince his readers of his sincerity. He has no intention, as he has already told them in iii. 1, of writing a testimonial on his own behalf. But he remembers that he has dangerous detractors at Corinth, about whom he will have more to say in chapters x and xi. He knows that their sense of values is totally wrong; they *glory in appearance, and not in heart*, the meaning of which is well brought out in Menzies' translation, 'they found their boast on their external position and not on what lies deeper'. He is anxious, therefore, that his loyal supporters at Corinth should remove the misrepresentations and the wilful misunderstandings of these misguided men. So he is giving them *occasion to glory* on his behalf. In other words, he is supplying them with an incentive to go proudly into the attack, and also with ammunition with which to fight, when they hear others running their apostle down. This interpretation is suggested by the word translated *occasion, aphormē,* which means both a starting point for an operation and the resources with which an operation can be launched.

13. In this difficult verse Paul seems to be telling the Corinthians that they should gladly rally to his defence if only because, in all his dealings with them, he had never shown any sign of wishing to please himself. They had seen him in many moods. Sometimes, as he spoke at their meetings under the stress of great spiritual emotion, they must have thought that he was *beside himself*, lost in ecstasy; but he had never sought glory for himself because of such experiences. Rather did they redound to the glory of God, the dative *to God* being probably a dative of advantage. At other times, and more frequently, he was quietly and soberly engaged in instructing and exhorting his converts—never, however, just to show what a good teacher and moralist he was, but always for their benefit, the dative of the original translated *for your cause* being also a dative of advantage.

Some commentators however construe *to God* as a dative of reference, giving the sense that Paul's spiritual ecstasy was purely a matter between himself and God, so that he would not have the Corinthians defend himself against his opponents by retorting that he had spiritual visions as well as they. On the other hand, his more sober activities, Paul is supposed to be saying, were to their advantage and therefore a cause for legitimate pride. It would seem, however, that both datives should be given the same significance, and that the two parts of the sentence should be taken as strictly co-ordinate. Paul's words are *or whether we are sober*, not 'but if we are sober'.

Other scholars consider that the reference in the phrase *beside ourselves* is not to excessive devotional fervour, but to extravagant self-commendation. Thus R. A. Knox paraphrases: 'I expect you think I must be mad, going on talking about myself like this; if so, treat it as an aside only meant for God; but if you can see sense in it it is meant for you.' But this exegesis is open to the same objections as the former; it regards the last part of the sentence as adversative, and fails to give a similar force to the two datives.

14. Paul now states the primary reason why he cannot live for himself. He is under the all-compelling constraint of Christ's love for him. This love holds him in its grip; so powerful is its influence that he has no choice but to live a life of loving service for others. It is interesting to notice that the word translated *constraineth*, *sunechō*, portrays in Lk. xii. 50 the sense of compulsion felt by our Lord as He fulfilled His vocation. 'I have a baptism to be baptized with', He said, 'and how am I *straitened* (RSV 'constrained') till it be accomplished!'

This obligation to live for others was laid upon the apostle when he was led to make two vital decisions about Christ's death. As the word translated *judge* in the original is an aorist participle, it would seem to refer to the time when these decisions were reached, probably soon after Paul's conversion.

In the first place, he came to learn how widespread were the effects of that single death. Christ *died for all*, i.e. for the innumerable company of those who would enjoy the benefits of His redemption. In a very real sense His death was their death. The translation *then were all dead*, though favoured by Chrysostom, is inaccurate because it construes the aorist *apethanon* as if it was an imperfect. It states, to be sure, what is true, viz. that if Jesus *died for all*, the inference must be that all were liable to the death which was the penalty of sin; but it is not this truth that Paul is now stressing. The aorist should be rendered 'therefore all died' as RV. Many modern commentators understand the reference to be to the mystical death which all who are 'in Christ' experience—the 'crucifixion with Christ' to which the apostle refers in Gal. i. 20. But, as James Denney points out,[1] 'what the apostle is dealing with here is something antecedent to Christian experience, something by which all such experience is to be generated and which is, therefore, in no sense identical with it.' It is, therefore, more probable that the apostle means that Christ's death was the death of all, in the sense that He died the death they should have died; the penalty of their sins was borne by Him; He died in their place; and this is why His love has such a compelling power over the believer, and engenders in him such undying gratitude.

15. The second conviction about the death of Christ to which Paul had been led by his conversion, was that for all who accept it in faith as an atonement made for *them* it puts an end to the unregenerate life, in which the old sinful self was regarded as the proper centre of reference, and begets a new life which is centred upon Another; not just upon *any* other but upon *One* other, the Lord Jesus Christ who *died for them, and rose again*. The resurrection cannot be divorced from the crucifixion in the atoning work of Christ, for, as Paul says elsewhere, 'He died for our sins, and rose again for our justification' (see Rom. iv. 25).

[1] *The Death of Christ*, Revised Edition, p. 84 (Tyndale Press, 1950).

j. The new creation (v. 16, 17)

16. Paul now illustrates how this determination no longer to
live for self but for Christ finds practical expression. The
particular judgment he had formed about the death of Christ
brought about a change in the way in which he regarded his
fellow-men. At one time he had estimated others, including
Christ, *after the flesh*, i.e. solely in the light of appearances and
superficial considerations. It is clear from the order of the
Greek words that Paul is speaking of the same 'knowledge
after the flesh' both with reference to Christ and to other men.
He is not saying that once he knew Christ-after-the-flesh (i.e.
the earthly Jesus), but that his way of regarding Christ was at
one time *after the flesh*. Hence it is almost certain that he is not
stating that he had once had first-hand knowledge of Jesus
when He lived on earth (a statement for which there would be
no other evidence) and that later he came to regard that
knowledge as inferior to his knowledge of Him as the risen and
ascended Lord. And it is equally improbable that he is saying
that in the light of his experiences as a Christian he substituted for such knowledge of the earthly life of Jesus as he may
have obtained from the original apostles a less limited, less
historically conditioned, and more mystical knowledge of
Jesus according to the Spirit, for there is no evidence that he
ever drove a wedge in this way between the Jesus of history
and the Christ of faith.

The right interpretation would seem to be that Paul admits
that in his pre-conversion days he had judged Jesus by external
considerations in the light of the prejudices of his upbringing,
and had concluded that it was impossible that one born in
such obscurity, living in such restricted circumstances and
dying such a humiliating death, could be the Christ that the
Jews were expecting. Consequently he had dismissed Him and
persecuted His followers. But *henceforth*, i.e. from the moment
of his conversion, he knew Jesus so no longer. Similarly, his
estimate of other men was now made *no more after the flesh*. That
was the method of the pseudo-apostles whom Paul has in

mind throughout this Epistle; and in so far as some of his converts at Corinth were showing a preference for them they were guilty of knowing others *after the flesh*.[1]

17. The particular change, of which Paul has just spoken, is one sign of the transformation that takes place in *any man* who is *in Christ*. 'Ye judge after the flesh', Jesus told the Jews. 'I judge no man' (in such a manner). No more does the man who is 'in Christ', because for him the *old things* have become *new*. The word *all* is not found in the most ancient MSS; but, whether it is in the text or not, Paul in the latter part of this verse is in fact saying, not only that the entire world of his experience changes for a man who is 'in Christ', but that because there *are* new men 'in Christ' the new order of things foretold in the prophet Isaiah has now become a reality (see Is. xliii. 18). Each man regenerated by the Spirit of God is a new creation, and a world in which such new creations exist is potentially at least a new world. So Menzies translates 'what is old is passed away, see! a new world has come'.

k. The ministry of reconciliation (v. 18–21)

18. By *all things* the apostle means in this context the whole of what is involved in the new order of which he has been speaking. This has been effected wholly by God, just as the original creation was entirely His handiwork. But Paul would not have been a new man in Christ, unless he had first been reconciled to God. God had, however, brought about that reconciliation *by Jesus Christ*, i.e. as Paul had learned at his conversion, by Christ's death on the cross. Man could not reconcile himself to God. He could not just say 'I will be a friend of God and no longer regard Him as my enemy'; for as a sinner it was man who was God's enemy and so banished from His presence. But the apostolic gospel was that God in His love had Himself brought about a reconciliation. This gospel had to be pro-

---

[1] In the commentary on verses 14–16 I have borrowed a few sentences from my sermon on 'The constraining love of Christ' printed in *The Narrow Way* (I.V.F., 1952). A fuller and more homiletic exposition of this passage will be found there.

claimed before it could be accepted; and, because Paul had been both called and empowered by God to proclaim it, his ministry could be accurately described as a *ministry of reconciliation*.

19. *To wit, that* translates the Greek *hōs hoti* which is probably the equivalent of the Latin *videlicet* with the sense 'What I mean is that'. In other words, Paul is here explaining more fully the implications of what he has said in the previous verse. He has been reconciled with God, because the reconciliation by God of sinful men to Himself, effected once and for all *in Christ*, has lasting effects. It is not applicable merely to one period or to one group of people, but to all the world. Whenever the *word of reconciliation* is proclaimed by those to whom God has committed it, and whenever it is appropriated by an individual sinner, whoever and wherever he may happen to be, that person is reconciled by God to Himself, and his reconciliation means that God no longer *imputes* to him his *trespasses*, i.e. He no longer counts his sins against him.

Paul is not in this verse explaining *how* this reconciliation is brought about by the death of Christ (a succinct statement about this is to be found in Rom. iii. 21–26); rather is he pointing out that the very existence of the divinely appointed ministry of reconciliation and the results that flow from it imply that that reconciliation, on which the entire new life of the Christian depends, has in fact been effected.

20. A minister of this word of reconciliation, i.e. a preacher of the gospel, can most properly be described as an *ambassador for Christ*, a title both proud and humble. For 'an ambassador', as Hodge pertinently remarks, 'is at once a messenger and a representative. He does not speak in his own name. He does not act on his own authority. What he communicates is not his own opinions or demands, but simply what he has been told or commanded to say. But at the same time he speaks with authority, in this case the authority of Christ Himself.'

God makes His appeal to men through such ambassadors. In His name they call upon men to accept the reconciliation made possible for them by the death of Christ, and so to enjoy the pardon, peace and power that such reconciliation alone can bring them. Paul now calls upon all at Corinth, who may hear this letter read out in the assembly and who are still at enmity with God, to accept the reconciliation open to them. But it should be noticed that he makes his appeal in a spirit of gentleness. *We pray you in Christ's stead.* Ambassadors engaged upon human affairs are chosen especially for their tact, their dignity and their courtesy, and because they are gifted with persuasive powers. The ambassadors for Christ should show the same characteristics. They must never try to bludgeon men and women into the kingdom of God, but must speak the truth in love, just because it is a gospel of divine love that they are commissioned to proclaim. It is surely significant that Paul, who was perhaps the greatest of all ambassadors for Christ, appeals to his readers 'by the meekness and gentleness of Christ' (x. 1).

21. The grounds on which Paul appeals to men to be reconciled to God are here condensed into a most memorable epigram, in which attention is directed to the great paradox of redemptive love. It is a paradox that baffles man's finite understanding, but nevertheless speaks irresistibly to his conscience when the Holy Spirit convicts him of sin and draws him to the cross. The one man who died for all *knew no sin*; His question 'which of you convicteth me of sin?' was unanswered when it was first asked, and it has remained unanswered ever since; the procurator Pilate could find no fault in Him, and a Roman centurion said He was innocent. And yet it was this sinless One that God *made . . . sin for us.*

It is not sufficient to regard the word *sin* in this context as equivalent to 'sin-offering', for although it is true that in the LXX of Lv. iv. 24 and v. 12 the word 'sin' by itself appears to have that connotation, this use is not found in the New Testament. Paul's words must mean that the sinless Jesus was made sin by being condemned to a criminal's death, and having to endure the ignominy and the punishment of the cross, solely that those who are sinners *indeed* might be acquitted by the holy God and be free to enter upon a new life pleasing to Him.

The apostle, we may be sure, does not mean that by 'making the sinless One sin' God the Father exercised any unloving compulsion upon God the Son. Both Persons of the blessed Trinity were at one in this divine redemption. The Father in His love sent the Son to be the Saviour of the world; and the Son showed His own love when He went willingly to the cross, and discharged at so great a cost the role delineated for Him by the prophet Isaiah. The great words of Is. liii. 4, 5 are indeed a better commentary on Paul's words than any human commentary could possibly be. 'Surely he hath borne our griefs, and carried our sorrows . . . he was wounded for our transgressions, he was bruised for our iniquities: the chastisement of our peace was upon him; and with his stripes we are healed.'

1. Paul's experiences as a herald of salvation (vi. 1–10)

1. In v. 20 Paul has spoken of the appeal that God makes to men through the preaching of His apostles. The work of evangelism is therefore a work in which man co-operates with God (see 1 Cor. iii. 9); so Paul can and must appeal to his readers to receive the salvation God offers. This reference back to v. 20 is missed in AV, where *also* is connected with *you* instead of with *beseech*. RV, more correctly, reads 'we intreat also'. By the use of the plural *we* throughout this section Paul identifies other heralds of salvation with himself, though the references are primarily to his own experiences.

The *grace of God* was most conspicuously shown in Christ's redemptive work as Sin-bearer, to which reference was made in the closing verses of the preceding chapter. There were, it would seem, some at Corinth who, while they may have heard the apostolic gospel, had not received it in such a way that it became a regenerating influence in their lives. They had not yet learned to say 'The Son of God who loved *me* and gave himself for *me*', and to allow that passionate conviction to perform its transforming work. Perhaps they still clung to the belief that they could achieve their own salvation; and to harbour any such delusion is to receive the grace of God *in vain*. Paul therefore beseeches them to welcome the good news upon which alone their salvation depends.

2. In this verse, grammatically a parenthesis, Paul underlines the urgency of his appeal in words taken from Is. xlix. 8. The original reference is to the help which God would give to His Servant in the day when salvation would be offered to the Gentiles. The Corinthians are now living in such a day of blessing. They are privileged to hear the gracious word of salvation proclaimed, and they are faced with the inescapable duty of either accepting or rejecting it. As Menzies comments, 'there was never such a day before—the accepted day for accepting the message, and for being themselves accepted and saved'. Few verses in the New Testament remind us more forcibly than this that the gospel must always be proclaimed as a matter of urgency, for the *accepted time* will not always be with us.

3. The apostle can make this appeal with confidence as well as with a sense of urgency, because he knows that his conscience is clear. No one can accuse him of preaching from unworthy motives, or of not having suffered for the doctrine he proclaims. Of himself and his fellow apostles it could never be said that they had received the grace of God in vain. The fact that Paul turns at once to what is in effect another defence of his ministry implies, as Denney rightly says, 'that there are people who will be glad of an excuse not to listen to the gospel, or not to take it seriously, and that they will look for such an excuse in the conduct of its ministers'. Paul forestalls any attempt at self-justification on the part of those who would seek to exonerate themselves in this way, by insisting that one of the primary concerns of his ministry is to avoid giving anyone the opportunity of making his conduct as a minister a ground for rejecting the gospel. As far as he was concerned, the effect of the message was not marred by the character of the man who gave it.

4, 5. The eloquent description given in the following verses of the ways in which Paul can commend himself, as all ministers of the gospel should be able to commend themselves,[1] is, as Menzies points out, 'not a mere effusion of the moment . . . the rhetorical arrangement, though it appears so natural and artless, is not without art'. In these two verses, nine different kinds of trials are enumerated in three groups of three, and the series is preceded by a reference to the supreme quality of *patience*, i.e. steadfast endurance, without which none of them could have been borne triumphantly.

In the first group, trials of a general nature are mentioned. *Afflictions*, *thlipseis*, include all experiences in which pressure—physical, mental or spiritual—is put upon him. *Necessities*, *anagkai*, refer to hardships of which no mitigation was possible. *Distresses*, *stenochōriai*, imply situations where there was no room to turn round and nothing but frustration, the exact opposite of the happy condition of the Psalmist described by him as 'being set by God in a large room' (see Ps. cxviii. 5).

The second group specifies particular sufferings inflicted upon Paul by other men. For *stripes* see the notes on xi. 24, 25, and for *imprisonments* those on xi. 23. Illustrations of *tumults* in which the apostle was involved can be found in Acts xiii. 50, xiv. 19, xvi. 19, xix. 29, and xxi. 30.

In the third group, the reference is to those hardships which Paul did not hesitate to inflict upon himself in the cause of furthering the gospel. *Labours* include all the manifold activities of his life as well as the manual toil by which he earned his living. For *watchings*, i.e. sleepless nights, see 2 Thes. iii. 8; and for *fastings* see note on xi. 27.

6. At the close of verse 5 there is what Denney calls 'a breathing place in the outburst of the apostle's feeling'. He now enumerates the spiritual graces which God enabled him to display as a minister of Christ, even amid the tribulation depicted in the previous verses. *Pureness* includes disinterested-

[1] *Ministers* is in the nominative in the Greek MSS. In Vulg. it is in the accusative. AV seems to have been influenced by Vulg. at this point.

ness and singleness of purpose as well as moral purity. *Knowledge* should be interpreted in this context as understanding of God's redeeming love revealed in Christ. By *longsuffering*, *makrothumia*, is meant patience with the obstinacy and stupidity of other people. *Kindness* is goodness in action, a reflection of the kindness of God shown even to the unthankful and the evil (see Lk. vi. 35). The presence of the *Holy Ghost* is seen in the supernatural power which Paul was able to exercise in his ministry (see 1 Cor. ii. 4 and 1 Thes. i. 5), and not least in *love unfeigned*. A very important aspect of this love (*agapē*) is a sincere, heart-felt concern to promote the true welfare of all the brothers for whom Christ died, however unattractive or unlikeable they may be. As such, it is foremost among the gifts of the Spirit, and a very real reflection of Christ's love on the cross.

7. By *the word of truth* is meant the proclamation of the revealed truth of the gospel, the task for which Paul had been directly commissioned by God (see Acts ix. 15). RSV, taking the genitive as one of definition, gives the possible but weaker sense 'truthful speech'. The apostle's preaching was not a merely human activity. Not only had its general content been divinely revealed to him, but the very language in which he presented it was given by the Holy Spirit, so that the *power of God* was continually apparent (see 1 Cor. ii. 1–5).

In the middle of this verse, the apostle makes another pause, which is indicated by a change of prepositions, for the following nouns are preceded by *dia* instead of *en*. He now describes in an eloquent crescendo some of the conditions under which his ministry is exercised, and some of the methods by which his spiritual warfare is waged. The armour with which he fights is *the armour of righteousness*. This genitive may be definitive, in which case the armour consists of the apostle's moral rectitude; or it may be a genitive of origin referring to the source from which the armour comes. If the latter is correct, *righteousness* would seem to be best interpreted in its technical sense of justification. Being justified in the sight of God, Paul is supplied by the Holy Spirit with the weapons with which he is able to fight—weapons for both attack and defence. *On the right hand* the sword of the Spirit lies ready for his use, and *on the left* the shield of faith affords him complete protection (see Eph. vi. 16, 17).

8. Sometimes the apostle's reputation in the eyes of men stands high; sometimes he is reckoned a person of no account and treated with disrespect. He is defamed, and he is praised; he is slandered, and he is honoured; he is criticized, and he is flattered. But, whatever men's estimate of him may be, he continues, undaunted, to 'fight the good fight of faith'.

In the series of contrasts beginning with *as deceivers, and yet true*, the apostle is probably illustrating some of the ways in which he is maligned and misunderstood by those who judged him superficially. RSV makes this clear by beginning the sequence of paradoxes with 'We are treated as impostors, and yet are true'. On the other hand, Denney insists that 'the apostle is not repeating what is said by others, but speaking for himself, and stating truth equally on both sides of the account'. It is difficult, however, to think of any sense in which Paul can have thought of himself as a deceiver even when speaking the truth.

9. Many of Paul's contemporaries no doubt dismissed him by saying, 'We have never heard of him'. He was a person, they felt, whom they could safely ignore. On the other hand, there were a few, upon whose minds and hearts his personality and his message had left an indelible impression; to them he was *well known*. To some he appeared a *dying* man, not only when persecution brought him to the threshold of death as at Lystra (see Acts xiv. 19) or more recently at Ephesus (see i. 9), but also in his constant exposure to dangers which might always prove fatal. He himself was conscious that mortal peril daily confronted him (see 1 Cor. xv. 30). But again and again, just when men were saying he was finished, he was seen (notice the insertion of the word *behold*) to possess fresh vitality and power. Suffering of various kinds frequently smote him with its chastening rod, but he could say with the Psalmist, whose experiences are in his mind as he uses the language of Ps. cxviii. 18, that such chastenings, so far from being signs of God's displeasure, as the ignorant might suppose, were occasions for the display of divine power, as God rescued him from the jaws of death.

10. To those whose outlook was almost entirely hedonistic and who identified joy with pleasure, Paul, with his self-mortification and constant denunciation of sexual vice, was a kill-joy, gloomy and morose. But he himself was aware of a perennial (notice the word *alway*) spring of joy in his heart; for, even in the midst of sorrow, he experienced an inward happiness born of Christian faith and Christian hope. *Alway rejoicing* himself, he could bid others rejoice in the Lord always (see Phil. iv. 4).

No less truthfully than Peter, Paul could have said, 'Silver and gold have I none' (Acts iii. 6), for the money that he earned by the sweat of his brow was barely sufficient for his maintenance. If there were times when he 'abounded', there were also times when he was 'in want' (see Phil. iv. 12). To many indeed he must have appeared a pauper. Nevertheless, though *poor*, he was rich with wealth unpriced. A worthy steward of the manifold grace of God, he had been entrusted with spiritual riches to be imparted to others; and all who received them entered into no less an inheritance than the kingdom of God.

There was no material property, Paul notes in conclusion, that he could call his own. Men might rightly consider him dispossessed, for the things that might have brought him earthly gain and worldly prosperity, such as privilege of race and social position, he had counted loss for Christ (see Phil. iii. 7). And yet, precisely because he was a joint-heir with Christ (see Rom. viii. 17), he had in his grasp the most wonderful possessions, which he had told the Christians at Corinth belonged to them as well. These possessions were none other than 'the world, life, death, things present and things to come' (see 1 Cor. iii. 21, 22).

IV. AN APPEAL FOR LARGE-HEARTEDNESS AND CONSISTENCY (vi. 11–vii. 3)

11. The direct address *O ye Corinthians* indicates the degree to which the feelings of the apostle have been stirred in writing the previous section. He rarely appeals to his readers by name; but just as resentment at the havoc wrought among the Galatian Christians by false teachers led him to cry 'O foolish Galatians, who hath bewitched you?' (Gal. iii. 1), and just as his gratitude to the Philippians for their generosity caused him to address them by name when he mentioned the subject (see Phil. iv. 15), so here his concern that his readers should understand how intimately he has unbosomed himself to them evokes the words *O ye Corinthians, our mouth is open unto you, our heart is enlarged.* He has spoken to them without reserve, and he feels that his heart has expanded in the process; for, as Chrysostom comments, 'As that which warmeth is wont to dilate; so also to enlarge is the work of love.' Largeness of heart was one of God's gifts to Solomon (see 1 Ki. iv. 29); and Isaiah prophesied that the heart of God's people would be enlarged to make room for the advent of the Gentiles (see Is. lx. 5). The heart of Paul, the apostle of the Gentiles, is sufficiently large for all his converts to be the objects of his affection.

12, 13. But this generous love of Paul has not been fully reciprocated by the Corinthians. While there is no lack of room for them in *his* heart, they do not always find room for him in *theirs*. They are *straitened* (RSV 'restricted') in their affections. So he appeals to them, as he would appeal to children who have an innate sense of fair-play, to requite his love *for a recompense* (RSV 'in return', the word *antimisthia* denoting an exact equivalent). This interpretation is justified by the absence of *my* in the original. Some commentators, however, maintain that Paul is not using what R. A. Knox calls 'school-room language', but is addressing the Corinthians as his spiritual children. In that case the insertion of *my* is necessary in translation.

14. The process of 'opening his heart' to his converts does not preclude the apostle from giving them, when necessary, urgent and severe warnings. One of the great problems of the Christians in a pagan city such as Corinth was to know how far they ought to segregate themselves from those who were outside their fellowship. In the first Epistle the apostle had advised them on this subject, and had advocated that, while every care must be taken to avoid idolatry, complete separation was unnecessary. It may well be that his advice had been received too lightly by the Corinthians; and in consequence he now insists with great emphasis that no *permanent* relationships must be formed between Christians and heathen. The danger of being *unequally yoked* (i.e. of compromising) *with unbelievers* was very real. The language of the apostle is influenced by the law 'Thou shalt not plow with an ox and an ass together' (Dt. xxii. 10), and by the prohibition of the hybrid breeding of animals (see Lv. xix. 19).

The standard of moral rectitude demanded of the Christians was as different from the immorality practised in the pagan world as *righteousness* is different from *unrighteousness* (RV, more accurately, 'iniquity', *anomia* meaning 'lawlessness'). On becoming Christians the Corinthians had emerged from a realm of *darkness* and were now *light* in the Lord (see Eph. v. 7). They had been called into the fellowship of God's Son (see 1 Cor. i. 9). The deeds of darkness which so disfigured paganism must therefore be cast aside (Rom. xiii. 12) as wholly incompatible with their Christian profession, for light and darkness cannot co-exist.

15. Paul now makes his rhetorical series of contrasts more personal. Not only are there abstract moral principles and standards which are mutually exclusive, but there are personal forces at work, stimulating men to action, which are directly opposed to one another. No *concord* is possible between *Christ* and *Belial*. Christ is the undisputed Head of all who call themselves by His name; and Belial (a Hebrew word meaning by derivation 'worthlessness' and used only here in the New

Testament for Satan) has sway over the various spirits which incite mankind to evil. Men must choose, so we read in one of the later Jewish books, either light or darkness, either the law of the Lord or the works of Belial (see *Testament of Levi* xix. 1). Similarly, *he that believeth* and the *infidel* (RV 'unbeliever') have no portion they can share together. They cannot 'throw in their lot' with each other.

16. It had been God's pleasure that His people should have, first in the tabernacle and later in the temple, a place set apart from all other places, to remind them of His continual presence with them, and to warn them against the cardinal sin of transferring the allegiance they owed to Him alone to the gods of the heathen that were but idols. Between *the temple of God* and *idols* there could be no possible *agreement*. Under the Christian dispensation, there is still *a temple of the living God*, but it consists of the whole company of Christian believers (see 1 Cor. iii. 17). This new temple retains the characteristics of the other tabernacle where God had been pleased to dwell. It is holy and dedicated, and must be kept a shrine fit for His presence. Paul does not hesitate therefore to apply words, first spoken with reference to God's presence with His people in the tabernacle in the wilderness, to His indwelling in the hearts of Christians (see Lv. xxvi. 11, 12). The same words formed part of the prophecy of Ezekiel, when he foretold that God would be present with His people after they returned from exile (see Ezk. xxxvii. 27).

17. Paul continues what is, in effect, a chain of Old Testament quotations, but inserts the word *wherefore* to show that he is now drawing practical implications from the great truth that the Christians are the temple of the living God. The older shrines were separated off from the world around them; so the Christians must be spiritually and morally withdrawn from the pagan society in which they have to live. Paul's appeal to the Corinthians to make this withdrawal is given in words originally spoken by God to His people through Isaiah when He called them out of exile. They were to leave behind them in Babylon everything that was unclean, taking only the sacred vessels of the temple, so that they might continue to be a people whom God could *receive*, i.e. whom He could look upon with favour (see Is. lii. 11). The Christian life is thus seen to be no barren renunciation, for the believer is separated from the world for no less a purpose than that he may enjoy friendship with God in the blessed company of other faithful people.

18. This truth now receives further illustration. The Christian Church is not only the temple of God, but the family of God. By becoming Christians men may have to regard as subordinate, or even to set aside completely, earthly family relationships; but, as Jesus so clearly taught, such loss would be compensated by new relationships in God's kingdom (see Mk. x. 29). God is first and foremost the *Father* of His people, and their relationship to Him is that of *sons and daughters*. In emphasizing this truth Paul seems to have in mind the promises made by Nathan to David about Solomon, 'I will be his father, and he shall be my son' (2 Sa. vii. 14), the words of Je. xxxi. 9 'I am a father to Israel, and Ephraim is my first-born', and the injunction of Is. xliii. 6 'Bring my sons from far, and my daughters from the end of the earth'. As these promises were made by *the Lord Almighty* (or, as the Greek *pantokratōr* more strictly means, the 'All-Sovereign') they are sure to be fulfilled.

vii. 1. In the original, *these* is very emphatic. The character of the promises, and the remembrance of who it is that made them must stimulate the Christian to play his part in satisfying the conditions of their fulfilment. He has a negative and a positive duty laid upon him. First, he must keep his entire personality, *flesh and spirit*, clean from everything that might defile it. As this task is accomplished by avoiding on specific occasions certain probable sources of contamination, the verb *cleanse* is in the aorist tense. But, secondly, there is the continual struggle, signified by the use of the present participle in *perfecting*, to bring to completeness that state of holiness, without which no man shall see God (see Heb. xii. 14). This is a life-long task to be achieved only if the *fear of God*, not the fear of men or the desire to please men, is the controlling emotion of the believer's life (see 1 Pet. i. 17).

2. *Receive* is a rather weak translation, and seems to have been influenced by Vulg. *capite*. Tyndale went deeper with the paraphrase 'understand'. The Greek *chōrēsate* means 'make room for' (see Mt. xix. 11 where it has exactly the same sense). RV and RSV 'open your hearts to us' is thus more accurate, though this might mean, in contemporary speech, 'speak freely to us'. Moffatt's 'make a place for me' is preferable. The apostle had chided the Corinthians in vi. 12 for being too restricted in their affections. He now renews the appeal, made to them in vi. 13, to open their hearts sufficiently wide for him to be an ever-present object of their love. There was no reason for restraint on their part, for there had not been a single instance where the apostle's teaching or conduct had had a deleterious effect. It was only his enemies who maintained that he was doing his converts positive harm, if not bringing them to ruin, by doctrine that in their view was subversive of morality, and who did not hesitate to insinuate that he used every opportunity to defraud (RV, better, 'took advantage of') them, not least by underhand financial dealings. That the latter charge was brought against him is clear from xii. 17, 18.

3. In speaking like this, Paul does not wish the Corinthians to feel that he is passing sentence upon them. To do that would be contrary to the tenor of his words in vi. 11–13, the purport of which, he now says, was that he would never exclude them from his affections even if he was dying, much less when he was alive and well and their interests were his daily concern. So Moffatt, 'You are in my very heart, and you will be there in death and life alike'; and R. A. Knox, 'Nothing in life or death can part us from you'. This is probably the right interpretation, though the Greek might mean that Paul is ready to share either death or life with the Corinthians. This meaning seems to lie behind AV and RV.

It is worth noticing that the words *I have said before* may be taken to imply that Paul is deliberately making a reference back to vi. 11–13 after what he is conscious has been an abrupt diversion. If this deduction is legitimate, it is an argument against the view that vi. 14–vii. 1 is an interpolation from another letter.

V. PAUL'S COMFORT AT THE NEWS BROUGHT BY TITUS (vii. 4–16)

4. So far from the apostle having cause to condemn the Corinthians, he is very confident about them, particularly for reasons that become increasingly apparent in the course of this section. Though the primary meaning of *parrēsia* is *boldness of speech*, often in the New Testament, and probably here, it has the more general meaning of 'boldness' or 'confidence'. Paul has already noted the frankness with which he has been speaking to the Corinthians. He now refers to the 'great confidence' (RSV) with which he can speak to others about them. The Greek *pros humas*, *toward you*, means here 'with reference to you'. His *glorying* on their behalf, i.e. his pride in them, is great. For, though they still have many imperfections, their recent attitude to the apostle, as confirmed by the report of Titus, has brought him in full measure the *comfort* he so much needs; and the joy, of which he had been so sorely bereft during the anxious period of waiting for news about them, was now overflowing.

5. Paul recalls the memorable meeting with Titus in Macedonia, first mentioned in ii. 13, where, somewhat abruptly, he had broken off the subject without giving any details about the news that Titus was able to give him, for he had felt an irresistible urge to pour out his heart in thanksgiving to God for the wonderful blessings that were always resulting from his ministry. He now recalls the restlessness which he felt on his arrival in Macedonia, probably at Philippi. In ii. 13 he had called this a restlessness of *spirit*; here he speaks of it as a restlessness of the *flesh*. There is no contradiction; for the *flesh* is here, as Plummer points out, 'the sphere, not of sin, but of suffering'. It is part of the frailty of human nature that it is subject to tensions and strains which have both mental and physical repercussions; and such strains are most acutely felt by hyper-sensitive souls such as Paul. It is not surprising therefore that Paul felt *troubled on every side* as he awaited Titus. We should probably not attempt to identify too specifically the references to these troubles. But commentators, from Chrysostom onwards, have usually supposed that by *fightings without* Paul is thinking of his conflicts with unbelievers, and that by *fears within* he is expressing his concern for his converts. He was always afraid that Satan might be trying to seduce them (see I Cor. vii. 5); and as he anxiously waited in Macedonia he was apprehensive that all might not be well at Corinth.

6. *Nevertheless* the coming of Titus had proved to be yet another occasion on which God showed that He did indeed comfort His people and have mercy upon the afflicted (see Is. xlix. 13). RV substitutes 'the lowly' for *those that are cast down*. RSV rightly restores 'the downcast', making it clear that the word *tapeinous* denotes the 'humiliated' rather than 'the humble'.

7. It was a real comfort to Paul to see his trusted ambassador Titus once again. But equally consoling was the knowledge that Titus himself had been comforted when he saw how the attitude of the Corinthians to their apostle had changed as the result of the painful letter and Titus' visit. The Greek *eph' humas*, loosely translated *in you*, makes it clear that this new attitude of the Corinthians was the basis on which his comfort rested. The threefold repetition of *your*, given an emphatic position in the original, also underlines this truth.

Titus was able to report to the apostle that the Corinthians were now showing an *earnest desire* to see Paul again, and to be restored once more to happy fellowship with him; they were *mourning* for their past behaviour, especially perhaps for the pain they had caused the apostle; and they were exhibiting a *fervent mind toward* (RV, better, 'zeal for') him, which no doubt expressed itself in a willingness to defend him against his detractors and to respond to his wishes. As Plummer well remarks: 'Previously the longing, lamentation and eagerness had been Paul's, and it was a delight to his emissary to find similar feelings in the Corinthians.' The result was that the joy that Paul felt at seeing Titus again was increased by the report that Titus had been able to give.

8. By a *letter*, a specific letter is meant. In the Greek the definite article is used. Hence RSV rightly translates 'my letter'. The letter in question is almost certainly not 1 Corinthians, but the subsequent 'painful' letter. Paul had known that this letter would cause distress; and so long as it was the right kind of sorrow, only good could result. There was a time, however, as he now confesses, when he was uncertain whether he ought to have written quite in the strain that he did, because he was ignorant of the nature of the sorrow it had caused. 'Regret' (RV) should be substituted for *repent* which is too strong a translation.

As there would seem to be nothing in chapters x–xiii, the writing of which could have caused Paul regret, it is unlikely that they are a part of this 'painful' letter. Some of the scholars who support this hypothesis admit this, and assume that the 'regrettable' parts were to be found in the portion of that letter which is now lost. Any regrets the apostle may have once harboured had quickly faded into oblivion, because he now understood that the pain it had caused was not the kind of pain that would permanently rankle, but a pain that would leave a blessing behind it when it had done its remedial work. The very letter now seemed remote from him—hence the reference to *the same epistle*, which should be rendered as in RV 'that epistle'.

The punctuation of this verse in both AV and RV is unsatisfactory. If it is adopted, the clause beginning *for I perceive* would appear to give the reason why Paul said he had made them sorry, and not the reason why he regretted having done so; and as Hodge rightly remarks, 'it amounts to little to say,

"I made you sorry, for I see I made you sorry" '. Much better sense is obtained if the words *Now I rejoice* in verse 9 are taken not as the beginning of a new sentence, but as the apodosis of a conditional sentence, the protasis of which begins with *Though I did repent*. A full-stop should therefore be placed after *I do not repent*; and the words *for I perceive . . . for a season* should be placed between commas, as giving the reason why Paul was caused regret.

Both AV *for I perceive* and RV 'for I see' translate the reading *blepō gar*, which, apart from the variant *blepō*, 'I see', was the only reading in the Greek MSS known to the makers of those versions. In the Vulg., however, the present participle *videns* is found; and Hort conjectured that the original Greek text also had the present participle *blepōn*. His conjecture has found remarkable confirmation in P.46, which alone of extant Greek MSS has this reading. Had it been known to the Revisers, they would almost certainly not have retained the unsatisfactory punctuation of AV. R. A. Knox brings out the sense that the adoption of the present participle enables us to find in the passage. 'Yes, even if I caused you pain by my letter, I am not sorry for it. Perhaps I was tempted to feel sorry, when I saw how my letter had caused you even momentary pain, but now I am glad; not glad of the pain, but glad of the repentance the pain brought with it.'

9. All sorrow that leads to *repentance* can truly be said to be *after a godly manner*. For a man repents when he turns to God, sees his conduct as God sees it, submits to God's judgment and asks God to forgive him. Sorrow for wrong-doing, which leaves God out of account, is merely remorse, that melancholy compound of self-pity and self-disgust. So far from healing and uplifting, remorse depresses and embitters. By divine over-ruling Paul's 'painful' letter, so far from causing the Corinthians to suffer damage at his hand, was the means by which they had received much blessing.

10. Although the order of the Greek words suggests that *not to be repented of, ametamelēton*, should be attached to salvation, better sense is obtained by connecting it with *repentance*. Hence RV, 'a repentance which bringeth no regret'. The difficulty of thinking that salvation could ever be a cause for regret would seem to be responsible for the Vulg. rendering of *ametamelēton* by *stabilem*, 'secure'.

All sorrow, whether it be due to disappointment, affliction, bereavement, or sin, is deadly in its operation so long as it remains unsanctified. In itself sorrow has no healing power. *Godly sorrow* (Moffatt, 'the sorrow that God directs') alone is remedial. The classical sermon of Francis Paget on 'The Sorrow of the World'[1] expounds its meaning with special reference to the particular sin called by the mediaeval Christian moralists *accidia*, 'a compound of depression, sloth, and irritability which plunges a man into a lazy languor and works in him constant bitterness'. This was regarded as one of the seven deadly sins; and because monks were particularly prone to it in the middle of the day, it was sometimes identified with 'the sickness that destroyeth at the noonday', of which the Psalmist speaks.

11. That *godly sorrow* is indeed salutary can be seen, the apostle asserts, in the beneficent effects it had upon the Corinthians. It made them concerned about the offence that had been committed in their midst. Instead of indifference there was an eagerness on their part to clear themselves of the guilt in which they were involved; *indignation* at the shame it had brought upon them; *fear* of the divine wrath to which they had become exposed; a *vehement desire* to see their apostle again; a *zeal* to promote his honour (see verse 7); and a readiness to mete out to the offender the 'punishment' (so RSV, instead of *revenge* and RV 'avenging') he deserved. The Corinthians had shown themselves *clear* (RSV 'guiltless') in this matter *in all things* (RSV, better, 'at every point', as the Greek is in the singular).

12. The effects of the 'painful' letter had indeed proved so

[1] To be found in the volume of sermons entitled *The Spirit of Discipline* (Longmans).

beneficial, that it could almost have been said that the primary object for which Paul had written it was neither the punishment of the offender nor the vindication of the offended party. But Paul is not saying, as the reader might at first sight suppose, that the latter objects were not present in his mind when he wrote. He is in effect using the common Semitic idiom which states as a contrast what in reality is a comparison. This can be brought out by translating 'not so much for his cause'. The most important object that has been achieved is seen in retrospect to have been almost the sole object that the writer had in mind, viz. that the care of the Corinthians for their apostle should be seen both by God and themselves in its true light. There is considerable confusion in the MSS at this point between the personal pronouns. AV, *our care for you* translates the reading found in Vulg. and many Greek MSS; but, though this thought has a parallel in ii. 4, it does not suit the present context. As Menzies says, 'The painful letter was written to make the Corinthians clearly conscious of the sentiment with which they did all the time regard him. That was to be done before God, in a marked and solemn manner, so that there could be no going back on it afterwards.' RV rightly follows the reading of B, P.46 and other authorities 'your earnest care for us'.

13. In the majority of ancient Greek MSS the word *de*, translated *yea, and*, is not found in this position, but introduces a new clause beginning with *in your comfort*. If this reading is followed then the opening sentence *Therefore we were comforted* should almost certainly be taken (as in RSV) as concluding the previous verse. Such a division of the text is further justified, when we notice that *in* does not accurately translate *epi*, which means 'over and above', and that the reading 'our' is better attested than *your*. What the apostle is saying is that, in addition to his own comfort caused by the report he has received about the Corinthians, his joy has been increased at seeing the joy experienced by Titus whose *spirit* had been *refreshed* by them. RSV therefore rightly begins a new paragraph with the words 'And besides our own comfort we rejoiced still more at the joy of Titus . . .'.

14. It is clear from this verse that Paul had boasted, i.e. spoken with pride, to Titus about the Corinthians, for *if* is not conditional but relatival, the meaning being, 'the boast which I made to Titus'. We may perhaps assume that before Titus set out on his fateful errand, Paul had encouraged him to think that he would find the Corinthians submissive; though the apostle had his own inner misgivings, which in love for his converts he kept to himself. His words had now been proved to be the exact truth, as true as the gospel truth which Paul had always proclaimed to the Corinthians so unequivocally.

15. Titus' affection for the Corinthians had become very great as the result of his visit. The comparative *more abundant* may well have a superlative force as so often in Hellenistic Greek. So Knox translates, 'He bears a most affectionate memory of you'. What Titus has treasured most is the obedience shown by every one of the Corinthians to the demands he had to make. They had, moreover, received him *with fear and trembling*, an expression which Paul uses of himself in I Cor. ii. 3, of Christian slaves in Eph. vi. 5, and of Christians generally in Phil. ii. 12. In all these cases it would seem to denote not nervous panic, but 'a solicitous anxiety lest love should fail in doing all that is required of us' (Hodge).

16. As the scribe may well have thought who first inserted the word *therefore* in the text followed by AV (it is omitted in all the ancient MSS), this verse forms the conclusion not only of the section which precedes it, but of the whole of the first part of the Epistle. A more impressive finale is achieved by the older reading which omits the inferential particle (as in RV).

For *I have confidence, tharrō*, RV (but not RSV) has 'I am of good courage'. Either translation is possible; but 'confidence' seems to fit the present context better. 'Courage' is preferred by those scholars who find here a reference back to x. 1, 2 which they regard as part of the earlier 'painful' letter.

In the light of the confidence that the apostle now has in the

Corinthians, he ventures to bring before them in the next two chapters the somewhat delicate question of the collection for the poor saints.

VI. THE COLLECTION FOR THE CHRISTIAN POOR IN JUDAEA (viii. 1–ix. 15)

The Christian Church inherited from Judaism the duty of almsgiving. Jesus assumed that His disciples would continue to practise it, but He stressed the importance of avoiding ostentation and self-righteousness (see Mt. vi. 1–4). After Pentecost, opportunities for the exercise of charity soon arose, as the Christians at Jerusalem seem, for the most part, to have come from the poorer classes. The unity of the believers was, however, threatened, when it was found that in the daily distribution of alms some distressed widows, perhaps because of linguistic difficulties or racial prejudice, were being neglected; and seven ministers were appointed especially to deal with this anomaly (see Acts vi. 1–6).

Paul was no doubt aware of the problem that had arisen at Jerusalem; and he was anxious that the members of the churches founded by himself should by systematic giving not only avoid being plunged into unnecessary poverty themselves, but should also be mindful of what they owed as Gentiles to the mother church at Jerusalem, and try to repay something of this spiritual debt by contributing from time to time to its material needs. The church at Antioch had done this, when the famine which swept across the world in the reign of the emperor Claudius brought additional distress to the Jerusalem Christians; and Paul himself had been one of the delegates of the church of Antioch on that occasion (see Acts xi. 27–30). In the Epistle to the Galatians he reminded his readers that the day of opportunity would eventually pass, perhaps quite soon, and that it was incumbent upon Christians to do good to all men, especially to those who had the same faith as themselves (see Gal. vi. 10). In 1 Corinthians, where we find the first mention of the expression 'the collection for the saints', Paul reiterates instructions for systematic giving which he says he has already laid before the Galatians. Each Sunday every member of the church is asked to put aside something for the fund, the amount to be conditioned by his earnings in the previous week, so that a substantial sum might be ready when the apostle came to collect the contributions of the various churches, and to make arrangements for their dispatch to Jerusalem by the hands of accredited representatives of the churches (see 1 Cor. xvi. 1–4).

A year or less had elapsed since the Corinthians had received these instructions, and during the interval much had happened which had not made it easy for the Corinthians to respond in any effectual way to the apostle's appeal. They had indeed made a start, but that was about all (see viii. 10, ix. 2). But now that the 'painful letter' had achieved its purpose, and the Corinthians were for the most part reconciled to Paul, the time was ripe for calling their attention once more to the great project of the collection, symbolical as the apostle considered it to be of the unity between Gentile and Jewish Christendom. The moment was also opportune, as he was soon to make a third visit to Corinth before setting out once again for Jerusalem. It is not then surprising that two whole chapters of this Epistle should be occupied with this subject, and that the writer should deal with it so thoroughly and with such insight that we have here what might be aptly called a philosophy of Christian giving, which has lessons to teach the Church in every age.

a. The example of the Macedonians (viii. 1-7)

1. The word mistranslated *Moreover* marks in effect a transition to a new section of the Epistle. It should either be left untranslated as in RSV, or be translated by some such word as 'Now'. *We do you to wit* is archaic, and we should substitute 'we make known to you' (RV).

If Corinth had been slow to respond to the apostle's appeal, the Macedonian Christians had given both generously and graciously. Their contribution, it would seem, was well-advanced, if not complete; and Paul feels that their example ought to act as a stimulus to the Corinthians. The liberality of the Macedonians is a visible expression of the divine grace they have received, for it is the Holy Spirit who inspires Christians not only to give spontaneously, and even more generously than their means would appear to warrant, but to give to people they have never seen, solely because they recognize that all believers are one in Christ. The words *bestowed on* mean literally 'given in' as RV.

All the districts of Greece north of the Isthmus of Corinth since 146 BC had constituted the Roman province of Macedonia; and the *churches*, to which the apostle refers, would seem to be those of Philippi, Thessalonica and Beroea. The liberality of the Philippians is underlined in Phil. iv. 15.

2. In addition to being extremely poor, the Macedonian Christians had recently been subjected to considerable persecution which had tested their faith. References to the suffering of the Thessalonian Christians under persecution are found in 1 Thes. i. 6, ii. 14 and Paul himself had suffered persecution both at Philippi (Acts xvi. 20) and at Thessalonica (Acts xvii. 5). Nevertheless, because of the grace of God that was in them, the Macedonian Christians were able to exhibit, even under persecution and in poverty, two of the loveliest flowers of the Christian character, *joy* and *liberality*. Christian joy arises from the sense of sins forgiven and from the assurance that the sinner now enjoys the favour of God; and Christian liberality springs from a heart conscious of the infinite generosity of God in giving His Son to redeem mankind. So great was the Macedonians' joy that it produced an abundant munificence; and the greater their poverty, the greater their liberality seemed to be. To them could be applied the words of Jesus about the widow who put her two mites into the treasury; they gave 'of their want' (see Lk. xxi. 4).

The Macedonians' poverty was due partly to the harsh treatment they had received from their Roman conquerors, who had exploited the rich natural resources of their land; and partly to the succession of civil wars which had been fought on their soil before Augustus became sole emperor.

The word translated *liberality*, *haplotēs*, means, by derivation, simplicity or single-mindedness; and it refers here, as in Rom. xii. 8, to giving which is uncalculating and free from ulterior motives.

3-5. In these verses Paul produces three direct and incontrovertible pieces of evidence to prove the liberality of the Macedonian Christians.

1. 'They gave' (RV rightly supplies this verb from verse 5) not only according to their ability, but even beyond it; and they gave without the apostle having to put any pressure upon them. Instead of *they were willing of themselves* read with RSV 'they gave . . . of their own free will'.

2. They urged the apostle not, as AV states, to receive their alms, but to allow them as an act of grace to have a share in the charity he was organizing. The words translated *that we would receive*, *dexasthai hēmas*, are poorly attested and should certainly be omitted. With their omission and the elimination of the words inserted in italics in AV, *take upon us*, the nouns *gift* (lit. 'grace') and *fellowship* become the direct objects of *praying*. What the Macedonians in fact had asked the apostle for was the favour and fellowship of this ministry, i.e. as RSV rightly translates, 'the favour of taking part in the relief of the saints'.

3. Their contribution was not a matter of alms only. Some financial aid the apostle had expected; but they had done more than this. They had dedicated themselves (*their own selves* is emphatic in the original) to the Lord, for such was God's will for them, and offered themselves to the apostle for any Christian service in which he might wish to use them. The word *first* is probably not used here in a temporal sense. Paul would assume that the Macedonians had already made that submission to the Lord without which there can be no Christian faith or Christian charity at all. But they had done something extra. In addition to giving their alms, they had placed themselves unreservedly in the apostle's hands for the service of Christ, and regarded this submission as a matter of

supreme importance. The significance of *first* is well brought out in Plummer's comment 'the crowning point of their generosity was their complete self-surrender'.

6. The connecting words *insomuch that* imply that as a result of the Macedonians' generosity and total commitment of themselves to the Lord, Paul is encouraged to take steps to bring about the completion of the collection among the Corinthians. He feels sure that He who had begun such a good work in them will enable them to bring it to perfection. He tells them therefore that he has *desired* (RSV, better, 'urged') Titus to revisit Corinth in order to bring about this happy result. Titus has not yet started out on this errand; the Greek aorist tense has here the significance of a perfect. AV *begun* does not bring out the meaning of the original, *proenērxato*, which implies that Titus had begun the organization of the collection at Corinth before something else happened, i.e. either before the Macedonians had started to make *their* collection, or, perhaps more probably, on a visit of Titus to Corinth some time previous to the writing of the present letter. This visit would seem to have taken place about a year before (see ix. 2); and it may be a legitimate inference that Titus himself was the bearer of I Corinthians in which Paul's instructions on this subject were given.

The AV translation *the same grace* implies that Titus is to bring to completion among the Corinthians the same divine grace as had been shown so conspicuously among the Macedonians. But the original means 'this grace'. RSV is therefore probably right in translating 'this gracious work'; for it is unlikely that Paul would say that Titus either could, or would bring to completion the grace which was essentially a gift of God (see Eph. ii. 8).

7. The apostle does not however make his appeal to the Corinthians solely by bringing to their notice as a moral incentive the example of the Macedonians. He also bids them remember the spiritual resources available for themselves. *Therefore* is a mistranslation of the Greek *alla*, which is adversative. Its force here is well brought out in Plummer's para-phrase, 'But there is another and a stronger consideration'. The Corinthians, as is clear from the first Epistle, had shown that they possessed many gifts of the Spirit; but hitherto generosity had not been among their more conspicuous virtues. An ungenerous Christian is, however, far from being a complete Christian. Yet there is no Christian virtue expressive of Christian love which a Christian cannot possess. *Ye abound in every thing*, the apostle reminds them, especially *in faith, and utterance, and knowledge*, i.e. in the power of understanding and giving expression to Christian truth; *in all diligence* (RV 'earnestness'), i.e. in vigorous Christian activity of all kinds; *and in your love to us*. In this last phrase a variant reading found in P.46, B and other ancient authorities, reverses the personal pronouns 'in our love to you' (RV mg). The literal meaning of the Greek expression used in both readings would seem to suggest the sense, 'the love which originates with you (or 'us') and finds a permanent abode in us (or 'you')'. In other words, the love of a Christian for a fellow Christian is a blessing and inspiration in the hearts of those who experience it. Because of the presence of these spiritual gifts in the Corinthians, the apostle feels justified in appealing to them to show in this matter of the collection (RSV 'this gracious work') a degree of liberality comparable to their other gifts.

b. The supreme motive for Christian giving (viii. 8–15)

8. No one can love to order, and no one can show liberality, which is an expression of love, to order. There must be an element of spontaneity in Christian charity; otherwise alms-giving degenerates into a work of law, as it tended to do in Pharisaism. Paul does not therefore dare to *speak by command-ment* in this matter. He assumes that the Corinthians have the gift of love, but he tactfully reminds them that love must express itself in action, just as faith must issue in works. And he uses *the forwardness of others*, i.e. the earnest zeal of the Macedonians, as an *occasion*, or opportunity, to *prove the sincerity* (lit. 'genuineness') of the love of the Corinthians.

9. This verse, though it is in the nature of a parenthesis, nevertheless refers to a most important truth of the Christian religion. Paul has just stated that Christian love must express itself in generous action. Here he underlines the truth that the example of Christ, and gratitude to Him for His infinite condescension on behalf of sinners, are the supreme motives for Christian charity. No one can be a Christian at all without knowing something of this condescension. Paul therefore assumes that the Corinthians have experienced it. *Ye know*, he says, *the grace of our Lord Jesus Christ*. The mention of the human name *Jesus*, together with the title assumed by Him during His earthly ministry *Christ* (omitted by B but almost certainly original), and also the exalted name to which He became entitled by His redemptive work (see Phil. ii. 11), *Lord*, is most impressive.

The *grace* in question was shown in the fact that *our Lord Jesus Christ . . . became poor*. The aorist tense of the verb suggests that it is the fact of the incarnation, rather than the conditions under which the incarnate life was lived, that is here uppermost in the apostle's mind. The Christ became poor in the act of becoming man. It was not so much in the lowly circumstances of the human birth, as in the fact that He should have been born at all, that the greatness of the condescension lay. *Though he was rich*, i.e. though He shared His Father's glory before the world was created (see Jn. xvii. 5), nevertheless He temporarily laid aside this glory in order to 'be found in fashion as a man'. He did not lay aside His divinity; for there is no doctrine of *kenōsis*, or emptying of His Godhead, to be found here any more than in Phil. ii. 7. In reading this verse the Christian cannot, however, forget the purpose of the incarnation. The Lord was manifested in human flesh in order to take away sin (see 1 Jn. iii. 5); and the taking away of sin involved His taking upon Himself the role of the suffering Servant, and being the Son of man who had nowhere to lay His head (Lk. ix. 58), and who was to die without a single possession; even the clothes He wore were stripped off Him by the soldiers responsible for His execution. Here was poverty indeed, and all for our sakes.

The purpose of this willing submission to poverty was that believers, who accept in faith the sacrifice made by Him on the cross for their sakes at such tremendous cost, should one day share the very glory which He had laid aside precisely in order that He might die the death by which alone He could redeem them. If this love of Christ, so magnanimous in its motive and so self-sacrificing in its execution, is an active force in the believer's heart, how unnecessary, the apostle implies, any *command* to practise almsgiving ought to be. What, without that love, might seem a cold moral duty has been transformed by it into a joyous privilege.

10. While the apostle refrains from giving a definite command in this matter, he does not hesitate to give specific advice. His opinion is that it is *expedient*, i.e. in the best interests of the Corinthians, to proceed with the collection (after *expedient* the infinitive 'to perform' should be supplied in sense from the next verse), because (the relative *who* has a causal sense) this is the only fitting conduct for men who, about a year ago, first started upon this enterprise. As Jesus said: 'No man, having put his hand to the plough, and looking back, is fit for the kingdom of God' (Lk. ix. 62).

The order of words in the expression *not only to do, but also to be forward* (lit. 'to will' as RV) is noteworthy. The reverse order would seem on the surface to be more natural, for willing precedes doing. The explanation would seem to be that the verb translated *begun before* implies that the Corinthians had a double priority over the Macedonians. Before the latter had even thought about taking part in the scheme, and before they had made a single contribution, the Corinthians had shown their eagerness in a very practical manner. There was, therefore, a double reason why they should not leave their work incomplete, particularly as it was their zeal based on their willingness to perform it, which had stimulated the Macedonians to action when the apostle had spoken to them about it (see ix. 2).

11. Because of the expediency mentioned in the previous

verse Paul does not hesitate to give what is in grammatical form a command, though he wishes it to be accepted as friendly advice rather than an order. The Corinthians must complete what they have begun. The will to achieve led to their initial activity, and the same will must now lead them to finish the work. They must give *out of that which ye have*, a literal but rather pointless translation (RV, better, 'out of your ability').

12. The standard of giving by which they will be judged will be conditioned by the extent of their means. What is most important is that they should have *a willing mind* (RV 'readiness'). The word translated *be first, prokeitai*, means, more probably, in this context 'be present'. Once the readiness to give is there (and if it is not, no giving is of any value at all), the only further point to be decided is the amount; and this depends on one consideration only, the financial resources of the donor. The widow who gave her two mites 'hath cast more in,' said Jesus, 'than all they which have cast into the treasury: for all they did cast in of their abundance; but she of her want did cast in all that she had, even all her living' (Mk. xii. 43, 44).

13, 14. The widow in the Gospels gave her full-day's wage in charity, an 'extravagant' act of self-sacrifice. Christians are always called upon to give generously, but not normally so generously as unduly to impoverish themselves or those dependent on them, especially if by such impoverishment all they are doing is to increase the ease of others beyond the demands of necessity. In verse 13 Paul points out the absurdity of almsgiving if giving to others (in this case, the Jerusalem Christians) means plunging the donors (the Corinthians) into distress. Charity must not be used for the encouragement either of laziness or luxury.

The principle to be kept in mind, as is stated in verse 14, is that of *equality*. There should be a mutual give-and-take, so that all men, particularly fellow-Christians, may be relieved of the burden of undeserved want. Owing to the fluctuating circumstances of human life, the rich of today often become the poor of tomorrow, and *vice versa*. When the apostle was writing, *now at this time*, the Jerusalem Christians happened to need the assistance of the Corinthians; but one day the position might be reversed. There is a sense, therefore, in which those who help others may be helping themselves, though this is very far from being the true motive for Christian charity.

15. The apostle closes this section of his appeal by citing an illustration from Scripture of the principle of equality stressed in the previous verse. When God gave the Israelites the manna in the wilderness (see Ex. xvi. 18) those who gathered more than others did not find that they were able to save more than they required for the satisfaction of their hunger; nor did those who gathered less than others, or what seemed inadequate for their own needs, find that those needs remained unsatisfied. It was as though God used the superfluity that some seemed to possess to make up the deficiencies of those who appeared to have too little. He would allow no one to hoard the gift He gave them. The same principle should be remembered, Paul insists, in the distribution of Christian charity.

c. The delegates of the churches (viii. 16–ix. 5)

16. In the furtherance of his efforts to bring about the completion of the Corinthians' contribution Paul is receiving staunch support from his trustworthy friend Titus, who has already rendered invaluable assistance in dealing with the difficult problems of the church at Corinth. It has already been suggested[1] that Titus may have been the bearer of 1 Corinthians and the probable initiator at Corinth of the collection. He had certainly carried the fateful 'painful letter'; and it was no doubt due to his efforts as mediator that a friendly relationship now existed between Paul and the Corinthians. God could indeed be praised for the way He had enabled Titus to further the work of His church at Corinth. In the translation *put*, AV follows the reading *donti*. If this reading is original, and

[1] See Introduction, pp. 16 f. and note on viii. 6 above.

the aorist participle is interpreted strictly, the reference would be to the initial movement of the Holy Spirit in the heart of Titus which enabled him to have *the same earnest care* for the Corinthians as the apostle had himself. This is a western reading, found in the Latin Vulgate, which survived in later Greek MSS, and is now seen to be very ancient by its occurrence in P. 46. The other reading *didonti*, followed by RV and RSV, is a present participle and draws attention to the truth that God who is the source of all goodness is continually reinvigorating Titus, so that his care for the Corinthians is always fresh and spontaneous.

17. This movement of the Spirit has led Titus not only to welcome Paul's *exhortation* (RSV 'appeal'), but also *being more forward* (RV 'being himself very earnest) *of his own accord* to volunteer to visit Corinth to further the apostle's designs. This visit is imminent at the time of writing. AV *he went* is a mistranslation, as it fails to notice that the aorist *exēlthen* is an epistolary aorist which should be translated as a present. Hence RSV, rightly, 'he is going'.

18. Titus is to be accompanied by two others to whom the apostle refers without mentioning their names. For *we have sent* read with RSV 'we are sending' for the reason just stated. As Paul refrains from mentioning the names of these men, it is somewhat idle to spend much time in an attempt to identify them. Jerome and Origen, wrongly supposing that the reference to *the gospel* was to a written Gospel, believed that Luke was the brother mentioned in this verse; and this interpretation is reflected in the Collect for St. Luke's day in the Book of Common Prayer. But it is certain that the Gospel of Luke was not yet in circulation, and that the reference must be to the praise earned by this brother in the churches, probably of Macedonia, as a preacher of the gospel. Many modern scholars, however, still adhere to this identification. Rendall, for example, believed it to be 'hardly short of demonstrable that this was none other than St. Luke'. His reasons were as follows:

In the list found in Acts xx. 4 of the envoys who eventually carried the collection to Jerusalem representatives are named from Beroea and Thessalonica, but none from Philippi. Nevertheless, the occurrence of 'we' in Acts xx. 5, 6 implies that Luke was among the party, and from this Rendall drew the conclusion that he was the representative of the Philippian church. Moreover, from the evidence of the we-sections in Acts, it is clear that the author is especially acquainted with events at Philippi; and the fact that in the subscription to the Epistle in some MSS Philippi is mentioned as the place where it was written affords some indirect support for the theory. Paul, however, had many helpers, and the identification of the brother in this verse with Luke cannot be regarded as anything more than a not improbable guess.

19. Whoever the brother of verse 18 may have been, he is going to Corinth not solely as Paul's representative, *not that only*, but because he has been duly elected by *the churches* (the plural would seem to indicate that he was not the delegate of Philippi or any single Macedonian church) to travel with Paul and his colleagues *with this grace*, i.e. as bearers of the collection. RV, following another reading 'in' instead of 'with', translates 'in the matter of this grace'. So RSV, 'in this gracious work'. The considerable support for the reading 'with' has been strengthened since the RV was made by the evidence of P. 46, and AV should therefore probably be followed.

The administration of this charity by Paul and the appointed delegates of the churches has as its primary object *the glory of the Lord*. Wherever believers reflect something of the generosity shown by God Himself (see verse 9), a little more of God's glory can be seen by men. *Same* should be omitted with RV. It is an inaccurate translation of *autou* which is not found in many of the oldest MSS. The second object of the administration of this charity is, according to the text followed by AV, to prove the Corinthians' readiness to give a practical expression of their love. Most ancient authorities for the text, however, have 'our' for *your*, as in RV and RSV. If this is correct, the reference is to the readiness of the apostle to 'remember the poor' as he had been asked by the Christian leaders at Jerusalem to do (see Gal. ii. 10). *Your* could easily have been substituted for 'our' in the light of viii. 11, and ix. 2, where it is the *ready mind* of the Corinthians to which specific attention is drawn.

20. Paul saw how important it was that the contributions of the churches to the fund for the poor saints at Jerusalem should be handled with scrupulous care, so that neither he nor his associates should be liable to the slightest suspicion of misappropriating other people's money. In dealing with this matter he combined the wisdom of serpents and the innocence of doves (see Mt. x. 16), and his example in this matter remains for all who are called upon to handle church finance. It is clear that he expected large sums to be contributed, for the word translated *abundance, hadrotēs* (RV 'bounty'; RSV 'liberal gift'), found only here in the New Testament, denotes munificent giving.

21. Unworldly people are apt in their innocence to suppose that, if only they are unconvicted by their conscience and their actions are unsullied in the sight of God, it does not matter whether they appear honest to their fellow-men. They tend, therefore, to minimize the importance of making it transparently clear to others that their actions are beyond suspicion. Paul, as Hodge well comments, 'recognized the importance of appearing right. It is a foolish pride which leads to a disregard of public opinion.' *Providing* is used here in its original sense of 'foreseeing'. RV avoids the archaism with 'we take thought for' and RSV with 'we aim at'. Paul tries to foresee and remove in advance any possibility of being misinterpreted.

22. The second unnamed delegate who is to accompany Titus to Corinth has been tested, and *proved diligent* on many occasions, and in a variety of matters. He is now *much more diligent* (RSV 'more earnest than ever') about the forthcoming mission to Corinth because of *the great confidence* he has in the

Corinthians. All that he has heard about them, perhaps from Titus since his return from 'the painful visit', has made him eager to undertake the task Paul has assigned him. Whether it is Paul or *our brother* who has confidence in the Corinthians, is not actually specified in the Greek text. Nevertheless, AV margin, followed by RV, is almost certainly right in supposing that it is the envoy's confidence that is implied. As Plummer rightly says, the sense supposed by AV text 'would require a pronoun to make it clear'.

23. Titus is already well known to the Corinthians. He has been Paul's *partner and fellowhelper* especially in his dealings with those somewhat troublesome converts. *Concerning you* is literally 'to you-ward' as RV. RSV paraphrases 'in your service'.

Of the two unnamed brothers, it is sufficient for Paul to say by way of commendation that they are *the messengers* (lit. 'the apostles') *of the churches*, duly appointed delegates, and that their character is such that it reflects *the glory of Christ*. He is glorified in them. Only a very small number of men were called to be apostles of Christ, and, comparatively speaking, only a few have been commissioned to undertake special acts of service for His sake on behalf of their fellow-Christians; but every Christian through the strength of the Holy Spirit can be *the glory of Christ*, reflecting to others something of the splendour of Christ Himself.

24. Paul concludes his commendation of the delegates with an appeal to his readers to give to these men practical *proof* of their love; and, in so doing, to justify his own *boasting* to others about his converts at Corinth. This demonstration of love is to be made *before the churches* (the preceding *and* has no ancient authority); this seems to mean, as Plummer paraphrases, 'as if the congregations to which they belong were present'. In any case, news of what the Corinthians did would soon travel back to the churches represented by the delegates.

ix. 1. Chapter divisions are not always found in the best places in our English versions, and the assignment of these words to the opening verse of a new chapter is somewhat mis-leading, for Paul, in fact, is continuing to speak about the delegates who are soon to visit Corinth. In viii. 24, he has urged the Corinthians to exhibit their Christian love before these men. How could they do this better than by proceeding at once with *the ministering to the saints* (RSV 'the offering for the saints'). They know this is what they ought to do, and they also know how they should do it. So Paul states in this verse that *it is superfluous* for him to repeat what he has already told them (viz. in 1 Cor. xvi. 1–4). The present tense of the infinitive '*to write*' signifies 'to go on writing'.

2. The apostle had been long aware of the readiness of the Corinthians to act in this matter; and during his stay in Mace-donia he has been saying in their praise *Achaia was ready a year ago*. 'Achaia' was the name of the Roman province which included the Isthmus of Corinth and all the land south of it. Paul flatters the Corinthians by this virtual identification of the province with their own city. The verb translated *was ready*, *paraskeuastai*, should probably be taken as a perfect middle, 'made preparations' (cf. 1 Cor. xiv. 8), rather than as a per-fect passive 'was prepared'. The Corinthians had not in fact been prepared *a year ago* in the sense that they had completed the collection and nothing more remained to be done, and Paul could never have made such a boast on their behalf. They had, however, begun to make preparation for it. M & M pro-duce evidence from the papyri to support the translation 'last year' for *apo perusi*, rather than *a year ago* or 'for a year past' (RV). If this is correct, it is not necessary to assume that twelve months have elapsed since 1 Corinthians was delivered and the Corinthians first began their preparations. Though they had not as yet done much to implement their plans, the apostle gave them full credit for what they had done, when speaking about them to the Macedonian Christians, with the result that *very many* (RSV 'most') of the latter had been *provoked* (RV, better, 'stirred up') to follow the Corinthians' lead.

3. Paul has already implied in verse 1 that there is no need for him to go on commending the collection scheme to the Corinthians. But there is great need for them to complete their contribution to it. This is the primary purpose for sending Titus and the brothers to Corinth. As before, *I sent* should be 'I am sending'. In some measure Paul's honour is at stake. It is not that he has given an untrue account to the Macedonians about the achievement of the Corinthians; but unless there is rapid progress at Corinth in the near future, his 'boasting' about them will be seen to have been unfounded and purposeless. On the other hand, if the Corinthians complete their contribution soon, Paul's pride in them will prove to have been justified. To say therefore that he is sending the brothers lest his boasting should be in vain, is the same as saying that he is sending them that the Corinthians may be ready. In other words, the last two clauses in this verse are strictly parallel.

4. The Macedonians, to be sure, will soon learn what the Corinthians have or have not done as the result of the mission of Titus and the brothers, for the apostle intends himself to pay a third visit to Corinth when he will be accompanied by some Macedonians. *If they come* does not imply that there is any doubt about Paul's companions on this visit; the Greek conditional particle often expresses (particularly in the New Testament where the language is influenced by Semitic idiom) something which will certainly take place (cf. Jn. xii. 32; 1 Jn. ii. 28). If the contribution is still far from complete when these Macedonians arrive at Corinth, Paul will feel a personal sense of disgrace 'for being so confident' (RSV) about them, even though, as he tactfully suggests, the disgrace would be more the Corinthians' than his. The AV *in this same confident boasting* translates a reading which literally means 'in this confidence of boasting'. 'Of boasting' is, however, omitted in the best authorities for the text, and RSV gives the correct sense.

5. Though time is short, the apostle is anxious to give the Corinthians as much time as possible for the amendment of their ways before he sees them again. This is why he is not himself going to visit Corinth with Titus and the brothers. He is leaving it to them to *make up beforehand* (i.e., as the verb *prokatartizō* implies, 'make up all deficiencies before I arrive') the *bounty* of the Corinthians. The word translated *bounty* (RSV 'gift'), *eulogia*, also means 'blessing'. Men can pray for a blessing on others, and they can, by their own actions, confer a blessing upon them. The Corinthian contribution will be a concrete blessing to those who will benefit from it. The words *whereof ye had notice before* translate the reading *prokatengelmenēn*, which has no ancient attestation. Even if this reading is followed, a far better sense would be obtained by supposing that notice of the bounty of the Corinthians had already been conveyed to *others*. The alternative reading *proepēngelmenēn* should, however, be followed as in RV 'your aforepromised bounty', or better, as in RSV, 'this gift you have promised'.

If the contribution of the Corinthians is really to be so substantial as to be worthy of being called a *bounty*, it will have to be a spontaneous act of charity, an uncalculating gift of generosity, not the grudging offering of men whose primary concern is how much they can get, and how much they can keep for themselves. *Not as of covetousness* is preferable to RV text 'not of extortion', and to RSV 'not as an exaction'. There is no suggestion that either the apostle or his envoys would ever apply force to extract from the Corinthians money they were unwilling to give. Contributions made under such duress would surely be better not made at all.

d. The blessings that await the generous (ix. 6–15)

6. The liberal giver, Paul proceeds to assure the Corinthians, need not fear destitution, for there is a real sense in which the generous man receives in return gifts out of all proportion to his own. This truth is emphasized in maxims found in the book of Proverbs. 'There is that scattereth, and yet increaseth; and there is that withholdeth more than is meet, but it tendeth to poverty. The liberal soul shall be made fat: and he that watereth shall be watered also himself' (Pr. xi. 24, 25). And 'He that hath pity upon the poor lendeth unto the Lord; and that which he hath given will he pay him again' (Pr. xix. 17).

Paul's language in this verse clearly echoes these sentiments; and he was probably familiar also with the saying of Jesus 'Give, and it shall be given unto you' (Lk. vi. 38). The unselfishness of Christian charity is not marred by remembering that such giving is in the best and the highest interests of the donor. As Hodge truly says: 'It is right to present to men the divinely ordained consequences of their actions as motives to control their conduct.'

7. Giving must be free and deliberate, not compulsory or casual. Each man must give *as he purposeth* (RV, following the better attested reading which gives a more accurate sense, 'as he hath purposed') *in his heart*; *not grudgingly*, i.e. not reluctant that he has to part with so much; *or of necessity*, i.e. not having as his main motive the consideration of what others will think about him if he refrains from giving. Both of these unworthy thoughts rob charity of its loveliness and its joy. They are, moreover, contrary to the revealed will of God as expressed in the LXX of Pr. xxii. 8, where we read that it is *a cheerful giver* that God blesses. The Hebrew of this passage runs 'he that hath a good (i.e. a beautiful) eye shall be blessed'. The eye was regarded in Hebrew thought as the window of the soul, through which a man's real motives were revealed. The LXX gives the general sense of the Hebrew while avoiding the peculiarly Semitic idiom of 'the eye'.

8. Generous giving for those who have little to give seems very hazardous; but the risk tends to be forgotten when the greatness of God's power is kept steadily in mind. All our resources, great or small, come ultimately from God; and *God is able*, Paul insists, to increase those resources. Where the generous spirit exists, God will provide the means by which it can be expressed. *Grace* is used here concretely; so RSV 'provide you with every blessing in abundance'. The result is that, furnished with the ability that God can supply, the charitable man will *always* have *all sufficiency in all things*. The word translated *sufficiency*, *autarkeia*, means first 'self-sufficiency', the feeling of being able to rely on one's own resources without

having to look to others or, as the Stoics said, without being
dependent on the caprices of fortune; and secondly, it describes
the contentment which such self-sufficiency engenders. The
noun is usually interpreted in the latter sense in 1 Tim. vi. 6,
'Godliness with contentment is great gain', though the sense
of that passage may be 'a life of piety lived by one who has
enough is wealth indeed'.[1] The cognate adjective *autarkēs* is
found in Phil. iv. 11, where the meaning seems to be 'I have
learned in whatever state I am therewith to be content'.
Here the apostle states that the believer by divine grace is
rendered self-sufficient and competent to meet the demands
made on his generosity, so that he *may abound to every good work*,
i.e. be able to perform it.

9. Paul now produces Scripture proof for the truth that the
giver shall be provided with the means of giving. In Ps. cxii,
after stating in verse 3 that the man who fears God will never
lack riches, the psalmist goes on to say in verse 9 that the
righteous man, who desires to express his righteousness in
beneficence, will never lack the means of doing it. *Righteousness*
is used here for 'almsgiving' (cf. Mt. vi. 1).

10. According to the late text followed by AV in this verse
Paul is praying a threefold prayer for the Corinthians. He
asks that God may *both minister bread for your food, and multiply
your seed sown, and increase the fruits of your righteousness*. In the
most ancient authorities for the text, however, the Greek verbs
are all in the future indicative; and this gives much the better
sense. It is the certainty of what God will do to which attention
is drawn. God is here described as the universal Provider in
language taken from Is. lv. 10. In keeping with the quotation,
'and bread for food' should accordingly be taken, as in RV, as
the object of *he that ministereth* (RV 'supplieth'). The beneficent
God, Paul tells the Corinthians, will *multiply your seed sown and
increase the fruits of your righteousness* (i.e. your liberality). Both
these clauses in effect say the same thing, for the last phrase,
taken from Ho. x. 12, refers to deeds of beneficence.

[1] See R. Falconer, *The Pastoral Epistles*, p. 154 (Clarendon Press, 1937).

11. As a result of this divine bounty, the Christian will find himself in full possession of what he needs for the exercise of charity. He will be *enriched in every thing to all bountifulness* (for the significance of the latter word translating *haplotēs* see note on viii. 2). But another great result will follow. The needs of the poor will be adequately satisfied, and, in consequence, many of them will be led to offer *thanksgiving to God* for the response of the Corinthians to the call to contribute given them by the apostle (the meaning of *through us*).

12. This further result is so important that Paul dwells on it again in this and the following verses. The glory of God is the goal of all Christian endeavour; and God is never more glorified than when His people offer Him the sacrifice of praise and thanksgiving. The supply of the material needs of the saints is, it is true, the immediate and very important purpose of *the administration of this service*, which probably means 'the service which the Corinthians will be rendering to God's people by their benefaction'. *Administration* translates *diakonia*, used in Acts xii. 25, of the 'ministry' fulfilled by Barnabas and Saul when they had carried the collection from Antioch to Jerusalem. *Service* translates *leitourgia*, a word used in the classical period for the public services rendered voluntarily by wealthy citizens at Athens. In Judaism it came to be used for religious service. Hence the English word 'liturgy'. It is used in Phil. ii. 30, in the same sense as in this verse.

But more far-reaching than this immediate result of the collection will be the *many thanksgivings unto God* which will be made by the grateful receivers.

13. The expression *by the experiment of this ministration* is better translated in RSV, 'Under the test of this service'. The meaning is that the service rendered by the Corinthians will afford an occasion for testing the sincerity of their religion, their *professed subjection unto the gospel of Christ*. It will also enable others to discover how far they have understood the unity that inevitably links together all who are living in communion with Christ. The translation *your liberal distribution* *unto them* assumes that *haplotēs* is used as in verse 11 in the sense of 'liberality', and that *koinōnia* means here 'contribution' (so RV, 'the liberality of your contribution'). It is possible, however, that the former word denotes here 'simplicity' or 'single-mindedness', and that the latter has its more common meaning in the New Testament of 'fellowship'. If so, what Paul is saying is that the Jerusalem saints will glorify God particularly for the signs of sincere Christian fellowship shown to them by the Corinthians in making their contribution. The latter interpretation is preferable, as it explains better the addition of the words *and unto all men*. The Corinthians' contribution is for the poor saints at Jerusalem only; but the fellowship which was expressed in it was, the apostle assumes, felt for all other Christians.

14. Paul has already said that the liberality of the Corinthians will cause many expressions of gratitude to ascend to God. It may be that in this verse he is saying, as AV seems to suggest, that a further result will be that the Corinthians will enlarge the circle of friends who will include them in their prayers. This would indeed be a very real and very full return for their generosity. This interpretation connects verse 14 closely with verse 12, and treats verse 13 as parenthetic.

It is however more probable that *kai* at the beginning of this verse should be translated 'also' rather than 'and'. So RV, 'they themselves also, with supplication on your behalf, long after you'. In other words, the reaction of the Jerusalem Christians to the fellowship of the Corinthians, a fellowship itself expressive of *the exceeding grace of God*, will be to express in their prayers an earnest longing to reciprocate it.

15. Commentators are divided as to whether by *unspeakable gift* is meant the grace of God bestowed on the Corinthians to which reference has just been made, and the blessed results of which will be especially apparent if they behave with generosity, or God's gift of His incarnate Son. A strong argument for the former interpretation, favoured by Calvin and many modern scholars, is that it underlines what is already present in the context. On the other hand, the epithet *anekdiēgētos* (found only here in the Greek Bible), meaning as it does a gift that cannot be adequately expressed in words, would appear somewhat hyperbolical if this is all that is meant. What the Holy Spirit was achieving in the world in the fellowship of the Christian Church was, to be sure, a very wonderful thing; nevertheless, Paul was given words in which to describe it, particularly when he was writing the Epistle to the Ephesians. It is, therefore, more probable, as Chrysostom suggested, that Paul, as he thinks of the divine grace bestowed on the Corinthians and remembers that all grace for the Christian flows from Calvary, because unredeemed men are strangers to that grace and because redemption was made on the cross and nowhere else, is led to burst into a cry of thanksgiving for the divine gift which inspires all gifts, the gift of God's own Son.

Plummer is scarcely justified in saying that a thanksgiving for God's supreme gift in sending His Son for man's redemption 'has only a very far-fetched connection with the context'. Hodge, more pertinently, remarks that 'it is Paul's wont, when speaking either of the feeble love, or trivial gifts of believers one to another, to refer in contrast to the infinite love and unspeakable gift of God in Christ to us' (cf. viii. 9; Eph. v. 2). Menzies, who prefers the former interpretation, nevertheless admits that 'the apostle is apt to be carried from an ordinary occurrence in the church to what is ultimate and supreme in God's counsels, and', he adds, 'it may be so here'. Strachan rightly insists that, while 'Paul has before him the vision of a united, world-wide Church, yet it is not merely the wonder of the picture, but its source which causes him to say "Thanks be unto God for His unspeakable gift". The unspeakable gift is Jesus Christ.'

We may therefore confidently assert that Paul concludes this extended discourse on the collection with a thanksgiving that 'God so loved the world, that he gave his only begotten Son' to be born and to die for mankind.

That Paul's appeal to the Corinthians did not prove to have been in vain is clear from Rom. xv. 26, 27, written some months later from Corinth. 'It hath pleased them of Macedonia and Achaia to make a certain contribution for the poor saints which are at Jerusalem.' It is however a little strange that in the list of Paul's fellow-travellers who eventually went with him to Jerusalem on the great errand of charity, while delegates are mentioned from the Macedonian churches and Asia, no representative is named from Corinth (see Acts xx. 4).

VII. PAUL'S APOSTOLIC AUTHORITY (x. 1–xiii. 10)

a. The weapons of his warfare (x. 1–6)

1. There is a definite break in the Epistle at the end of chapter ix as the apostle turns to deal with the recalcitrant minority at Corinth who, in contrast to the great majority of the Corinthian Christians, have not been loyal to him but are listening all too eagerly to the specious claims of certain false shepherds who have intruded into the fold of the Corinthian church. As it is *Paul's* authority which they have questioned, he abandons the plural of authorship in this verse, dissociates himself from Timothy (see i. 1), and makes a purely personal appeal to this group of dissentients—*I Paul myself beseech you*. Similar personal appeals are to be found in Gal. v. 2, Eph. iii. 1, and Phm. 19.

Paul is appealing to those who have been accusing him of being *in presence base among* them but *bold toward* them when absent, i.e. of showing a spirit of bravado when writing letters to them at a distance, but of exhibiting a pathetic cowardice in their presence. The word translated *base*, *tapeinos* (RV 'lowly', RSV 'humble') is sometimes used to describe a noble virtue (see Mt. xi. 29), but here it has the derogatory sense of 'faint-hearted'. Similarly, the word translated *bold*, used in a good sense in verse 6, here denotes the audacious effrontery of the coward when no danger is present. In view of their estimate of Paul's character his opponents were not in the least disturbed by the prospects of a further visit from him. As it had been before, they said, so it would be again. Since the main purpose of 2 Corinthians is to prepare the way for this third visit of the apostle to Corinth, he makes it clear at the outset of this section that it is always incumbent upon him as an apostle of Christ to have in mind in his ministry *the meekness and gentleness* of Him whom he is commissioned to serve. Jesus bade men come to Him precisely because He was 'meek and lowly in heart' (Mt. xi. 29); and it was said of Him that a bruised reed He would not break and smoking flax He would not quench (see Is. xlii. 3 and Mt. xii. 20).

Meekness, prautēs, is essentially an inward virtue, a grace of the Christian who is prepared to accept the discipline of God without dispute or resistance, remembering that He often uses the insults and injuries of evil men for the chastening and purifying of His people. The meekness of Jesus was preeminently shown in His submission to the wrongs inflicted upon Him in the discharge of His ministry as God's suffering Servant.

The word translated *gentleness, epieikeia,* is used by Aristotle to describe the clemency exercised by the judge who is good as well as just, and who recognizes that circumstances alter cases and that adherence to the strict letter of the law may sometimes result in the perpetration of moral wrong. This quality was displayed by God very often in His dealings with Israel; and the cognate adjective is found in LXX of Ps. lxxxvi. 5, and is translated in the English versions 'ready to forgive'. A supreme instance of the 'gentleness' of Jesus in this sense is found in the story of the woman taken in adultery (see Jn. viii. 1–11). In the only other passage where the word occurs in the Greek Testament it is used, as often in the papyri, somewhat conventionally by an inferior official paying a compliment to a higher authority whom he is addressing. 'I beg you', says Tertullus to Felix, 'in your kindness to hear us briefly' (Acts xxiv. 4, RSV).[1]

2. Paul regards it as axiomatic that a true minister of Christ should always use gentle methods in seeking to win the submission of men to the Saviour, and that they should employ

---

[1] For a fuller discussion of these two words see R. C. Trench, *Synonyms of the New Testament,* sections XLIII and XLIV. The sermon on 'Forbearance' by Francis Paget in *Studies in the Christian Character* should also be read.

more severe methods only as a last resort. He is most reluctant to use severity, and so he appeals to those who are confounding his gentleness with timidity, so to behave that he may not have to exhibit in person at Corinth the 'boldness' which they have been saying he displays only when there is no one present to see it. He is confident that he has the right as an apostle to exercise his authority with such forcefulness that if it does not command respect and obedience it will be to the eternal loss of the disobedient; and, if necessary, he is determined to show *that confidence* at Corinth without any fear of consequences in opposing those who so wilfully misinterpret him as to think of him as walking *according to the flesh.*

The exact nuance of this insinuation is not entirely clear. Hodge, following Chrysostom, gives to the expression *according to the flesh* the sinister meaning it so often has in the Pauline letters, and supposes that Paul's opponents 'regarded the apostle not only as an ordinary man, but as acting under the control of his corrupt nature, governed by selfish or malicious feelings, and relying on himself'. With this interpretation most modern commentators agree; and it would appear to be reflected in the RSV translation 'who suspect us of acting in worldly fashion'. Calvin, on the other hand, seems to have supposed that Paul's opponents took notice only of externals, and despised him for not excelling in the more conspicuous and showy endowments by which they endeavoured to commend themselves to their supporters. But, while this would seem to be the meaning of 'according to the flesh' in v. 16 (see note), the expression when accompanied by the word 'walk' seems to refer either to moral behaviour, or, as in x. 3, to the frailty and infirmities of life in the human body.

3. Paul admits that his apostleship in no way renders him superior to human infirmity. He is no superman, but has to *walk in the flesh* as all other men. But in the exercise of his apostleship, which involves him in a spiritual campaign in which he is always on active service, he is not at the mercy of the instincts of corrupt human nature, nor does he have to rely on his own human resources. Frail human being though he is, as a man in Christ he is empowered by the Holy Spirit. Here lies the permanent source and the unfailing supply of his supernatural strength and courage.

4. As his warfare is spiritual, so the weapons with which he fights must be those bestowed by the Spirit. *Carnal* weapons, such as human cleverness or ingenuity, organizing ability, eloquent diatribe, powerful propaganda, or reliance on charm or forcefulness of personality, are all in themselves quite unavailing in the ceaseless task of *pulling down* the *strongholds*, in which evil is entrenched. Such carnal weapons may win superficial or temporary victories, but it soon becomes evident that evil has not been driven from its fortress. The only weapons adequate for the struggle come from God, and He alone enables them to be effective. The Greek expression, meaning literally 'mighty to God', is translated by av *mighty through God*, i.e. 'rendered powerful by God' (so also rsv, 'have divine power'); and by rv 'mighty before God', i.e. 'mighty in God's estimation' or 'mighty for God's service'. The Christian will always be fighting a losing battle against temptation if he tries to fight against evil in his own strength. 'Not by might, nor by power, but by my spirit, saith the Lord of hosts' (Zc. iv. 6).

5. In this verse the enemy is seen to be impersonal. The warfare is not against 'flesh and blood' (see Eph. vi. 12), but against invisible and intangible spiritual forces which invade human nature and insinuate devilish thoughts into men's minds. Hodge defines *imaginations, and every high thing that exalteth itself against the knowledge of God* as 'the opinions or convictions of those who set themselves and the deductions of their reasons against the truth of God'. That truth has been made known partly in the world of creation and more clearly in the Christian gospel. The language used by Paul would seem to refer especially to the subtle philosophic arguments, the cunning devices, and the relentless cruelty with which these godless opinions are given expression. But, as the spiritual warfare continues to be waged (verse 5 is grammatically connected with verse 3, throwing verse 4 into a parenthesis) these strongholds of evil are penetrated, and *every thought* is brought *into captivity to the obedience of Christ*. One of the most astonishing and undeniable arguments for the truth of the Christian religion, and for the omnipotence of God, is the fact that, when faced with the gospel, which is a scandal to the human intellect and folly to proud, unregenerate men, some of the most subtle of human intellects have been led to render submission to the Saviour. Many of the wisest have been content to become as fools for Christ's sake, and not a few of the 'freest' of thinkers have surrendered their 'freedom' to become slaves of Him who took upon Himself the form of a servant.

6. Paul's main desire as an apostle and minister of Christ is to be used as the means by which men are led by the Spirit to render voluntary submission to Christ. But where there is perverse resistance to his ministry and deliberate attempts are made to undo his work, and where gentleness on his part is persistently being misconstrued as weakness, he is ready to *revenge* (RV 'avenge'; RSV 'punish') *all disobedience*. He has the power of passing sentence on such offenders; and, whether the effects of such sentence will be immediately evident (as in the case of Peter and Ananias and Sapphira, Acts v. 1–10) or not, it is a sentence of eternal significance. 'This vengeance', commented Calvin, 'is founded on Christ's word "whatsoever ye shall bind on earth shall be bound also in heaven".'

But the apostle is most anxious not to give the impression that the taking of such drastic action is anything except the last step in the exercise of his apostolic powers. He would never have them forget that to bring others into the obedience of faith is the primary and absorbing aim of his life (see Rom. i. 5, xvi. 26). This is probably why, in this verse, he adds the rather difficult words *when your obedience is fulfilled*. Calvin, in commenting on Jn. xx. 23, finely says: 'As the embassy of salvation and of eternal life has been committed to the apostles, so, on the other hand, they have been armed with vengeance against all the ungodly, as Paul teaches in 2 Cor.

x. 6. But this is placed last in order, because it was proper that the true and real design of preaching the gospel should be first exhibited. That we are reconciled to God belongs to the nature of the gospel; that believers are adjudged to eternal life may be said to be accidentally connected with it. Hence Paul, when he threatens vengeance against unbelievers, immediately adds, "after that your obedience shall have been fulfilled", for he means that it belongs peculiarly to the gospel to invite all men to salvation, but that it is accidental that it brings destruction to some.' Hodge brings out the same point when he says: 'Paul would not resort to severity until all other means have failed, and until it had become fully manifest who among the Corinthians would submit to God, and who would persist in their disobedience.'

b. Paul's consistency (x. 7–11)

7. There are two inter-related difficulties of exegesis in this verse. (i) The verb *blepete* can be taken either as imperative or indicative; and, if indicative, can be construed either as a statement or a question. Three translations are, therefore, possible 'Look on', 'You look on', or 'Do you look on?'. (ii) The expression *ta kata prosōpon*, translated *things after the outward appearance*, can be taken to mean 'the things that lie before your face', as in x. 1, and Gal. ii. 11, or 'the things that merely appear on the surface', as in v. 12.

If the verb is imperative, the sense must be 'look at what lies before you', for Paul would scarcely urge anybody to form their judgments merely by externals. On the other hand, if it is indicative, Paul would appear to be reprimanding those whose sole criteria for assessing others were their personal appearance or their more flashy achievements. This would seem to be the meaning of AV. The RV rendering 'Ye look at the things that are before your face' is not very lucid, but presumably means 'You confine your gaze just to what you can see without going any deeper'. On the whole, RSV, 'Look at what is before your eyes', is preferable. Paul is justifying the severe language he has been using by inviting all the Christians at Corinth to look at the existing situation there, and to see whether, in fact, there are not people among them whose attitude to the apostle accords with what he has said in verse 2. One particular individual might seem perhaps to be especially in Paul's mind, for *any man* could mean 'a certain man'. It is probable, however, that more than one person was attacking Paul's apostleship and for a variety of reasons, not least, as is made clear in the remainder of this verse, because in their view *they* were commissioned by Christ and he was not.

All Christians can claim to be *Christ's*, but this is not the sense here; nor is the phrase to be understood with reference to members of the 'Christ-party' at Corinth mentioned in 1 Cor. i. 12. It is Paul's opponents who are in his mind throughout this section. They attacked his apostleship, not least on the ground that they were superior apostles. For reasons best known to themselves they were certain that they had Christ's authority, that they had been sent by Him, and that they were equally as important as the original Galilean apostles, while Paul was not. In this verse Paul does not categorically deny their claims. He is content quietly to point out that if any of them is personally convinced about the validity of his own credentials, then he cannot deny to him, Paul, the right to say, equally as the result of personal conviction, that he too is Christ's. Personal conviction cannot be accepted as their prerogative, but not his. But it is subjective evidence. In addition, Paul can produce more convincing objective testimony than they could. He hints at this in the following verse, and speaks more directly about it elsewhere (see iii. 2, xii. 12 and 1 Cor. ix. 2).

8. Paul here insists that, even if he were to *boast somewhat more* than he has previously done about his apostolic authority, he could do so without any sense of shame due to exaggeration or false pride. For the facts spoke for themselves. It was evident that in the exercise of his apostleship supernatural powers had been released, which were particularly effective in building up converts in their faith. As a result the church was growing in harmony and peace. The *authority* which the Lord had given Paul had been used, and was being used, *for edification*. On the other hand, the assumed authority of the false apostles was equally clearly being used for *destruction*. It was dividing the body of Christ.

9. But, while Paul could with justification elaborate upon the nature and extent of his apostolic authority, he refrains from doing so because, as he here ironically suggests, he is writing a letter, and he would not like to seem as if he wanted to terrify his readers by his letters! For this was precisely what his opponents were asserting to be the main purpose for which he wrote them. The allegation was absurd; for, had it been true, the apostle would have been guilty of a suicidal inconsistency. The authority that the Lord had given him was for *edification*; and young converts are not edified by terrifying letters!

10. The damaging criticism that a different Paul was to be heard speaking in his letters from the Paul whose voice could be heard when he visited Corinth, was being circulated, perhaps by a particular individual, if the reading 'he says' found in almost all the Greek evidence is followed in preference to *say they* found in B and the Latin and Syriac versions. The variants are comparatively unimportant. It is more important to notice that these opponents were speaking the truth, when they said Paul's letters were *weighty and powerful*. As Menzies remarks, we have here 'a valuable testimony to the impression the Epistles of Paul at once produced when they were written; they were felt to be grave and important utterances, and they acted effectively, as they were intended to do'. This characteristic they have never lost.

His opponents were indeed right in their assessment of the power of Paul's letters; but they were wrong in supposing that he dare not act with the vigour and courage that characterized his written words. Their statement that *his bodily presence* was *weak* is not, as it has sometimes been taken to be, a reference to the apostle's personal appearance or physical condition; and we cannot deduce from it any evidence to help us in forming a portrait of him. His opponents were criticizing his general deportment. He writes boldly enough, they were saying, but he is a feeble person when it comes to taking action. Similarly, his manner of speech when he was addressing audiences at Corinth left much to be desired. By the standards of Greek rhetoric to which they were accustomed, it was *contemptible*. Other audiences would appear to have reacted somewhat differently to Paul's eloquence. The natives of Lystra called him Hermes, because he was the chief speaker (Acts xiv. 12). But, as Plummer comments, 'Paul had not the brilliance of Apollos, and he did not keep Eutychus awake' (see Acts xx. 9).

11. *Such an one* does not necessarily refer to a single individual; the expression could be used of anyone who might bring a charge of inconsistency against the apostle, such as that mentioned in the previous verse. The words *will we be* are not found in the Greek text, where the clause is devoid of any verb. RV supplies 'are we' from the early part of the sentence. If the future tense is inserted, the apostle has in mind his forthcoming third visit to Corinth; if the present, he is drawing attention to a permanent feature of his conduct. His behaviour when he is present with his converts is always consistent with what he says to them in letters when he is away from them.

c. Paul's appointed sphere of service (x. 12–18)

12. The apostle has been accused by his opponents of cowardice. He here makes an ironical confession that in one matter he is indeed a coward! He will not dare to class himself among, or to compare himself with those who make self-commendation, unsupported by any corroborating evidence, their title to fame. Such people measure their achievements by the degree to which they add to their own self-importance or gratify their instinct for self-assertion. In this they *are not wise*, which is a Greek way of saying 'they are utterly foolish'.

The last words of this verse *are not wise* and the opening words of verse 13 *but we* are omitted in the main authorities for the western text and in the Latin Vulgate; and this reading is accepted by some modern scholars, including Moffatt. If it is followed, the word translated *they*, *autoi*, becomes the subject of *will not boast* in verse 13, and must be translated 'we ourselves'; and the meaning is well brought out in Moffatt's translation 'they belong to the class of self-praisers; while I limit myself to my own sphere, I compare myself with my own standards, and so my boasting never goes beyond the limit'. If this western reading is original, we should have to account for the rise of the longer reading by supposing, as Strachan suggests, that some copyist had difficulty in realizing that Paul is speaking ironically and regarded it as inappropriate that an apostle should speak of comparing himself with his own standard. He, therefore, inserted the words found in AV and RV. On the other hand, as the longer reading is so well attested, and the shorter reading could easily be due to an accidental omission, one of the commonest causes of variations in MSS, it should be accepted. It gives, moreover, a good sense. The point Paul is making is that self-praise is dispraise. The false apostles, *measuring themselves by themselves, and comparing themselves among* (RV 'with') *themselves, are not wise.* But Paul does not, in fact, boast of himself by any self-made standards; relying on the grace of God, he accepts from Him an appointed sphere of labour to which he strictly confines himself.

As a point in favour of the unity of the Epistle it should be noted that Paul seems to have these same false apostles in mind in the earlier part of the letter, when he implies in iii. 1 that he does not need letters of commendation as some others do, and when in v. 12 he suggests that he must not commend himself, as presumably others were doing.

13. If the apostle is to boast at all about his apostolic achievements, his boasting, unlike that of the false apostles whose conceit knows no bounds, will be kept within clearly defined limits. It will not be *without measure* (RSV 'beyond limit'). God has *distributed* (RV 'apportioned') to him a *rule*; He has marked out for him a sphere of service as a minister of the gospel, and Paul will boast only of what comes within the limit of that sphere.

The word translated *rule, kanōn,* is interesting. Originally meaning a reed, it came to be used primarily of anything straight enough to be used for the purpose of measuring, and secondly for what the ruler measures off, and so, in an ethical sense, for the 'rules' or principles which keep people's lives 'straight'; for what is measured off by the ruler tends to become the rule. In this verse, it has the sense of the area measured out and allotted to Paul (so RV 'province', RV mg. 'limit'). Our word 'canon' is a transliteration of the Greek. The canon of Scripture means the books ruled off as different from all other books and possessing a unique authority. A Canon of a cathedral is one who lives in accordance with the rules or statutes of the cathedral. Similarly, in full accordance with the sphere of work marked out for him by God, the apostle has certain 'rules' which control his missionary activities. Two of the most important of them are (1) he is the apostle of the *Gentiles* (see Acts ix. 15; Rom. i. 5), a principle that was recognized by James, Cephas and John at Jerusalem (see Gal. ii. 9); (2) he must not build on other men's foundations (see Rom. xv. 20). In other words, he is a pioneer missionary to the heathen. Corinth came within his rule, for he was the first to preach the gospel there (see 1 Cor. iii. 6), and it was predominantly a Gentile church.

14. In the light of this, the false apostles had no authority for ministering at Corinth other than that which they had arrogated to themselves. It was they who were stretching themselves beyond measure, not Paul. Priority of service gave Paul a prior claim to the loyalty of the Corinthians. The Greek translated *we are come, ephthasamen,* is better rendered, as in RV mg. and RSV, 'we were the first to come'.

15. Corinth, Paul repeats, came within the *measure* or province assigned him by God. If it had not been so, he could never have conducted a successful mission there; and it is of his achievements there, accomplished by the power of the Spirit, not *of other men's labours* that he boasts. The false apostles were talking as though they had been the first to preach the gospel at Corinth, and were claiming it as their rightful sphere of jurisdiction. This was preposterous. As Calvin comments: 'Paul reproves more freely the false apostles, who, while they had put forth their hand in the reaping of another man's harvest, had the audacity at the same time to revile those who had prepared a place for them at the expense of sweat and toil.'

It was to the great discredit of a small section of the Corinthian Christians that they had given these men a hearing; and Paul does not propose to venture further afield in missionary work until their *faith is increased*. He hopes indeed to preach the gospel in places beyond Corinth, but only so soon as the state of affairs at Corinth permits. However loyal most of the Christians had now proved themselves to be, he will not risk leaving behind him in their fellowship a festering sore which might lead to more serious trouble. Hence the tremendous importance of his forthcoming third visit to the city, to prepare the way for which is the main purpose of this Epistle. If the Corinthians, *all* of them, prove loyal to him on that occasion, then his hope may be fulfilled, and he may be able to visit other parts of the world which would appear to come within the sphere allotted him. The Corinthians have the opportunity of opening up this wider sphere of activity for the apostle. He can be *enlarged* by them *abundantly*, the words *by you* (lit. 'in you') implying 'with your assistance'. RSV 'that . . . our field among you may be greatly enlarged' does not seem to give good sense, as the enlargement of Paul's field of service at Corinth is not the point at issue.

16. The places Paul has in mind as possible spheres for further evangelistic work are not specified; he refers to them vaguely as '*the (regions) beyond you*'. It is a legitimate inference from Acts xix. 21, and Rom. xv. 22–24, that the reference is to a visit to Rome preliminary to a mission to Spain. One thing

Paul here asserts very clearly; even if he visits places (such as Rome) where other Christian missionaries have been at work, he will never appropriate to himself the fruit of other men's labours. He will *not boast in another man's line of things made ready to hand.* We should substitute for this unusually clumsy rendering the more lucid RSV 'without boasting of work already done in another's field'.

The fact that Paul had this prospect of further missionary activity in view when he was at Ephesus, and that the expression *the regions beyond you* would be an apt description of Rome and Spain in a letter written from Ephesus, does not afford an adequate argument for assigning this part of 2 Corinthians to an earlier letter written from Ephesus. Rome and Spain were just as much 'beyond Corinth' to a writer composing a letter in Macedonia as to a writer at Ephesus.

17, 18. Paul has used the word 'boast' a good deal in this section, having been led to do so by the extravagant boasting of his opponents. He is, however, most anxious that it should not be thought that he himself is indulging in any self-glorification, as though what he had achieved had been due entirely to himself. His first and permanent reaction when confronted with the blessings that resulted from his missions was 'To God be the glory'. Never did he yield to the temptation that besets every evangelist, to over-estimate his own powers, or to pay undue attention to the applause and flattery of men. The divine injunction, given through the prophet Jeremiah, had sunk deep into his soul. 'Let not the wise man glory in his wisdom, neither let the mighty man glory in his might, let not the rich man glory in his riches: but let him that glorieth glory in this, that he understandeth and knoweth me, that I am the Lord' (Je. ix. 23, 24); and it is from this passage that Paul takes the words recorded in this verse. To have *God's* approval is his sole desire; and the only things in which a Christian, and especially a Christian evangelist, can truly glory without being unworthy of his profession, are the things which God has already done or has promised to do through him.

In verse 18, the apostle seems to turn his thoughts once more to his opponents. The primary difference, he implies, between them and him is that they commend themselves, and in so doing disqualify themselves from receiving God's approbation, while he seeks divine acceptance as one who, because he gives glory to God, is one whom God can commend. It is significant that, when Paul and Barnabas returned from the first missionary journey, they rehearsed to the church at Antioch *not* what they had done, but 'all that God had done with them, and how he had opened the door of faith unto the Gentiles' (Acts xiv. 27). So far from glorifying in himself, Paul is able to say of his ministry: 'I have therefore my glorying in Christ Jesus in things pertaining to God. For I will not dare to speak of any things save those which Christ wrought through me, for the obedience of the Gentiles, by word and deed, in the power of signs and wonders, in the power of the Holy Ghost' (Rom. xv. 17, 18, RV).

d. Paul's claims on the Corinthians' loyalty (xi. 1–6)

1. Paul is very conscious that it is no business of an apostle, or indeed of any Christian, to praise himself. Such self-commendation is only justified, in the present instance, because his affection for his converts is so great, that he will go to almost any length to prevent them from becoming the dupes of unscrupulous men, and to keep them loyal to Christ. In his case, at any rate, self-praise is not in the least prompted by vanity and conceit. He prays, therefore (for his wish *Would to God* is in effect a prayer), that all at Corinth will *bear with me a little in my folly*. The tense of the verb in this clause, imperfect middle, implies the sense 'Would that you could bear with me *now*'. Rendall is, therefore, inaccurate in supposing the apostle to mean 'Would that you *had* borne', i.e. on Paul's last painful visit to Corinth. The verb translated *bear with me* could be taken as indicative (as RV mg.) as well as imperative. If the former, the sense is 'Yet my prayer is not really necessary, for you do, in fact, bear with me'. If the latter, then Paul makes a fervid appeal to the Corinthians, as in RSV, 'Do bear with me!'.

2. Paul's converts ought to be able to bear with him, because, as he states here very definitely, his 'folly' is prompted by the kind of *jealousy* which a lover feels for his beloved. Such jealousy is *godly*, because it is felt by God Himself, when His people, so often described in the Old Testament as standing towards Him in the relationship of a wife to her husband, give their allegiance to other paramours.

The apostle naturally feels this jealousy for the Corinthians, because it was through his ministry that they ceased to be heathen, and became part of God's people by being 'wedded' to Christ. Paul had not brought them into such a relationship with himself that they could say they belonged to *him*. Everything he had done had been with the sole object of enabling them to say that they belonged to *Christ*. They were his work 'in the Lord' (see 1 Cor. ix. 1). He had begotten them 'in Christ Jesus' (see 1 Cor. iv. 15). But just as a father is not only responsible for having brought his daughter into the world, but also 'gives her away' to her husband, so Paul had *espoused* the Corinthians *to one husband*. By adding the word *one* Paul stresses the truth that, just as the marriage relationship is exclusive, so believers in Christ owe an exclusive loyalty to Him. Here lay the danger of the false apostles. Although, as yet, only a few of the Corinthians had become a prey to their sinister tactics, there was a risk that they might distract the church as a whole from its loyalty to Christ.

Paul looks forward to the Lord's return, not least because then the time for the marriage of the bride will have come (see Rev. xix. 7), and he will have the inestimable privilege of presenting his converts, the church of God at Corinth among them, as *a chaste virgin to Christ*, the heavenly Bridegroom. This was the ultimate purpose for which he had betrothed them to Christ. Indeed, it was the ultimate purpose for which Christ died; for He 'loved the church, and gave himself for it . . . that he might present it to himself a glorious church, not having spot, or wrinkle, or any such thing; but that it should be holy and without blemish' (Eph. v. 25–27).

3. The apostle's jealousy for the Corinthians is the product of a well-grounded *fear, lest by any means your minds should be corrupted from* (i.e. 'corrupted so as to be diverted from') *the simplicity that is in Christ.* Single-hearted devotion to Christ is easily destroyed. This is implied in the parable of the sower when, after the word of God has been heard, 'the cares of this world, and the deceitfulness of riches, and the lusts of other things entering in, choke the word, and it becometh unfruitful' (Mk. iv. 19). The danger of the false apostles lay in their false estimate of Jesus, and in their desire to improve upon, by making their own additions and subtractions, *the simplicity* of the gospel. Whenever the Christian religion ceases to be purely Christ-centred, and no longer draws its inspiration and power solely from Him, who died for our sins and rose again for our justification, it is in danger of being corrupted. When men, beguiled by false philosophies of human origin, look anywhere else except to the cross of Calvary for salvation, or when they are misled into thinking that the rites and ceremonies of the Church are in themselves the means of salvation, then the simplicity that is in Christ is lost.

Many ancient authorities, including P. 46, add the words 'and the purity' (RV) after 'simplicity'. If this reading is original, then the marriage symbolism is sustained, and the thought is that the chaste virgin must beware of losing her purity during the interval between her betrothal and her presentation to her divine Husband as His bride. These words may, however, have been an explanatory addition made under the influence of the cognate adjective *chaste* in verse 2; they are, in fact, redundant, for, when the simplicity that is in Christ is lost, the purity of the believer's life is in danger of being lost as well.

The weapon of all false teachers is *subtilty*; this is why Satan tempted Eve in the form of the most cunning of all God's creatures, *the serpent*. And the sphere in which this weapon does its deadly work is the human imagination; for once the *minds* of men are corrupted, their whole personality is rendered impotent to do good. From Eve onwards, the human heart has been prone to be deceived by those who, appearing to have wisdom, insinuate by plausible suggestions and arguments the most destructive of all lies that men and women are not inextricably bound by the limitations of their creaturely estate; that they are not under an imperative duty to recognize and obey their sovereign Creator, but that they have it in their power to break their restrictive fetters, and give free expression to their instincts unbound by any revealed moral law. So the serpent suggested to Eve that by disobeying the divine command she might become 'as God' (see Gn. iii. 1–6). The explanation of the permanent predicament in which man finds himself, always resenting his position as a creature, is here stated to lie in the initial deception of Eve by the serpent. (See also 1 Tim. ii. 14.)

4. The particle *For* would seem to connect this verse in sense with verse 1 rather than with verse 3. In verse 1, Paul appealed to the Corinthians to put up with his 'self-boasting'. This ought not to be unduly difficult, he now somewhat ironically implies, at any rate for those of them who give such a splendid reception to the preachers of doctrines very different from those taught them by their own apostle.

This interpretation depends upon accepting as the true reading *anechesthe*, found in P. 46, B, and the first hand of D. This is a present indicative and means 'you put up with him'. The alternative reading *aneichesthe* is an imperfect indicative, and means 'you would be putting up with him'. This latter reading gives the impression that *he that cometh* is a hypothetical person who has not yet been seen at Corinth; but, as the verbs in the rest of the sentence are in the present indicative, this is unlikely. AV, translating a slightly different form of the second reading *eneichesthe*, gives the unfortunate rendering *ye might well bear with him*; and RV, translating the first reading, is equally misleading with 'ye do well to bear with him'. Both these versions give the impression that the Corinthians would be, or are, doing a good thing in tolerating these teachers; and they miss the irony of the passage. Any serious connivance by Paul at what the false apostles were teaching would be clean contrary to the spirit of Gal. i. 8. We need then some such translation as that of Menzies 'you put up with that finely'.

The somewhat satirical expression *he that cometh* perhaps carries with it the implication that, whoever these false apostles may be, they have no more authority for intruding into the Corinthian church, than the malevolent shepherds, mentioned by Jesus in Jn. x. 5, had for breaking into the fold for the purpose of plundering the sheep. What some of the Corinthians had been so ready to listen to from the lips of these impostors was nothing less than *another Jesus*. Paul does not say 'another *Christ*', for these apostles seem to have accepted Jesus as Messiah; but their interpretation of the ministry of Jesus was so utterly contrary to what Paul had given, that for all practical purposes their Jesus was another person. In listening to the presentation of a purely human Jesus the Corinthians might be inspired, Paul admits, by *some* sort of spirit; but such a spirit was very different from 'the Spirit of him that raised up Jesus from the dead' (Rom. viii. 11) which they had inevitably received (*elabete*) when they became believers. Similarly, there might be *some* good news in what they heard from these newcomers, but it was assuredly not the gospel of Christ crucified proclaimed by Paul, which the Corinthian Christians had voluntarily accepted (*edexasthe*) at the outset of their Christian life, the gospel that all who accept in faith the sacrifice made for them by Christ on the cross are reconciled to God and restored to fellowship with Him.

5. The interpretation of this verse depends upon the meaning given to the expression *the very chiefest apostles*. If this is a reference to the apostles who were 'pillars' of the Jerusalem church (see Gal. ii. 9), as most older commentators understood it to be, Paul recognizes the leading position which these men hold in the Church, but claims that he has as much right to be obeyed as they have, because he too has been divinely commissioned for his work, endowed with the gifts necessary to perform it, and vindicated by the success that has accompanied it. In this case, the connecting particle *For* links the verse in sense with verse 1, and Paul is giving another reason why the Corinthians should bear with him in his 'folly'. He is, he asserts, entitled to the respect to which the leading apostles are entitled, because he is *not a whit behind* them.

On the other hand, most modern commentators regard *the very chiefest apostles* as an ironical reference to the false apostles at Corinth. Hence the RSV translation, 'these superlative apostles'. If this is correct, then the verse is connected in sense with verse 4. The Corinthians are wrong, the apostle is saying, in tolerating these men, as some of them do, in view of the far superior claims of their own apostle. This interpretation should almost certainly be accepted. Not only does it suit the context, but it helps to explain the occurrence of the strange word *huperlian*, a rare compound of the preposition 'beyond' and an adverb 'exceedingly', to describe the consummate conceit characteristic of the apostles in question. Paul may well have himself coined this word, found also in xii. 11, for the occasion.

This verse cannot then be used, as it has so often been used in the past, either in the debate about the primacy of Peter, or as evidence for an alleged conflict between Paul and the older apostles.

6. In one respect alone does Paul admit his inferiority to the 'extra' apostles who are troubling the Corinthians. He is, compared with them, *rude in speech* (RSV 'unskilled in speaking'). The word translated *rude, idiōtēs*, meant originally a private person unconcerned with public affairs; and, as the Greeks were politically minded, not to be concerned with them was considered reprehensible, and so the word came to have a contemptuous flavour. Later, it was used for those who, because they lacked technical or professional training, tended to dabble in a subject or an occupation in a rather amateurish manner. Paul uses it in 1 Cor. xiv of the ordinary person who lacks an understanding of the special spiritual gifts, on which the Corinthians tended to set such a high value. Peter and

John were dubbed *idiōtai* (Acts iv. 13) because they had not had the specialized training in biblical exegesis enjoyed by the Rabbis. Paul here admits that he had had no training in professional rhetoric. He is an apostle, not an orator. An exponent of the gospel did not need, he would have claimed, to be a rhetorician, for the Spirit enabled him to give spiritual expression to spiritual truths (see 1 Cor. ii. 13, RSV mg.). It was the truth he taught that mattered most. What he will not admit is that he is unskilled *in knowledge*. The mystery of Christ had been fully revealed to him and fully expounded by him (see Eph. iii. 4, 5, and cf. 1 Cor. ii. 6–11).

Paul had made clear to the Corinthians his knowledge *in all things* necessary for the understanding of God's redemptive activity. We should adopt the reading of the most ancient authorities, *phanerōsantes*, active (RV 'we have made it manifest'), rather than the passive *phanerōthentes* found in the later MSS and translated by AV, *we have been made manifest*. The meaning of the AV text would seem to be that, however deficient he might be in rhetorical skill, in all other respects Paul had been manifested to the Corinthians as possessing the qualifications of an apostle. According to the RV text the meaning is that, so far from lacking knowledge of divine truth, the apostle has manifested it to the Corinthians in all its aspects.

e. Paul's pride in being self-sufficient (xi. 7–12)

7. Paul cannot be called to task for any failure to discharge what must be the primary duty of an apostle, viz. to expound the truths of the Christian revelation. Perhaps, however, he now suggests, objection could be taken to his apostleship on the ground that he had *committed an offence* (RV 'sin') *in abasing* himself by preaching the gospel *freely* (RV 'for nought'; RSV 'without cost'). It is clear from 1 Cor. ix. 4–15 that Paul's refusal to claim at Corinth the right, fully recognized in Scripture, of being supported by those to whom he preached the gospel, had been used by his opponents as a ground for invalidating his apostleship. He now rather tentatively suggests that some might again be wishing to bring up this accusation.

During his stay at Corinth he had earned his living as a tent-maker, but the false apostles who had succeeded him received pay for their 'services'. Paul could in a sense be said to be *abasing* himself by forgoing what was a legitimate privilege. Working night and day with his hands might seem an un-dignified occupation for an apostle. But what was his real motive? If it had been lack of loving care for the Corinthians, or a sense of self-sufficiency which was too proud to allow itself to be ministered to by others, then indeed he would be guilty of *an offence*. But so far from this being the case, his real motive was that the Corinthians *might be exalted*, i.e. that their attention might be concentrated solely on what the apostle was saying, and not on any material advantage he might be getting for saying it, so that they might be raised up from the death of sin unto a life of righteousness, and enjoy the exalted status of sons of God who were joint-heirs with Christ of the glory of the Father. Was *this* a *sin*?

8, 9. To enable Paul to be completely independent of Corinthian support, while he lived at Corinth, he had allowed *other churches* to make up the sum which the Corinthians might have legitimately been asked to contribute. In a sense, this *taking wages of them* was almost, Paul admits, a species of 'robbery' on his part, for, while these other churches could reasonably have been asked to maintain Paul when he was ministering to *them*, it was not incumbent upon them to pay his expenses when working at Corinth.

There was a time, the apostle states, during his stay at Corinth when the supply of money received from other churches, by which he supplemented the income that resulted from the pursuit of his trade, became exhausted. But even then he was *chargeable to no man* (RV 'not a burden on any man', the verb *katanarkaō* meaning 'to cause numbness by pressing heavily on someone') at Corinth, for *the brethren which came from Macedonia supplied* the additional amount required. This seems to be the force of the double compound in the verb *prosaneplērōsan*. The occasion of this Macedonian generosity must have remained in the memory of the Corinthians. It may, with confidence, be identified with the return of Timothy and Silvanus to Corinth, mentioned in Acts xviii. 5. The former had come from a mission to Thessalonica and the latter, most probably, from a mission to Philippi.

By the words *in all things I have kept myself from being burdensome unto you* Paul implies that in other matters, as well as those relating to finance, he has been anxious to be under no obligation to them.

10. It is clear that Paul had no hard and fast rules about receiving gifts from his converts. From the Macedonians he accepted contributions, but he persistently refused to allow the Corinthians to support him. As long as he worked *in the regions of Achaia*, he here solemnly asserts, *no man shall stop me of this boasting* (RSV 'this boast of mine shall not be silenced'). The verb translated *stop, phrassō*, is a very strong one. In the LXX it is used of damming a river in Pr. xxv. 26; and of barricading a road in Ho. ii. 6. Paul uses it in Rom. iii. 19, when he states that the indictment in Scripture of those who flout the divine law is made that 'every mouth may be stopped', i.e. that all possible excuses may be silenced.

11, 12. The reason for Paul's unflinching determination in this matter is not any lack of love for the Corinthians. He is able to call God to witness the truth of that—God who alone can fully discern the secrets of the human heart. What really determines his attitude is the presence in Achaia of men who snatch at any opportunity for maligning him, and who would be the first to say that he preached the gospel for the sake of filthy lucre. As he had told the Corinthians in a previous letter, he would rather submit to death than render himself open to such a charge.

The last words of verse 12 *that wherein they glory, they may be found even as we* are difficult. The probable meaning is brought out in RSV, 'to undermine the claim of those who would like to claim that in their boasted mission they work on the same terms as we do'. In other words, these 'superlative' apostles receive pay for their work, and they would like this difference between themselves and Paul to be eliminated by Paul behaving as they do, so that they may be on an equality with him.

f. The real nature of Paul's opponents (xi. 13-15)

13. The fundamental reason why the apostle is apprehensive about the influence his opponents may have upon his Corinthian converts, and why he himself would rather die than do anything which might in any way place himself upon their level, is stated in the forthright utterance of this verse. These men share with Satan, the arch-deceiver, his supreme characteristics of treachery and cunning. They are *false apostles*, claiming to be what they are not, for they have none of the marks of men commissioned by Christ and endowed with His Spirit. They are *deceitful workers*, for, however busy they may be in supposedly Christian activities, they are in fact serving not Christ but themselves, though posing as His ministers. They pretend to be enthusiasts for Christ's cause, but they are only acting a part. The meaning of the word rendered *transforming themselves* is that, however much they may change their outward appearance and manner, they remain fundamentally the same.

14. This behaviour of the false apostles ought not, Paul now asserts, to come as a surprise to those whose eyes are open to the methods adopted by the prince of evil and his satellites. In disguising themselves in this way they are imitating Satan who, consummate hypocrite that he is, poses as one of the highest and purest and most intelligent of God's creatures, *an angel of light*. While there are references in Jewish literature to Satan adopting the role of an angel, no passage has been found where he is portrayed as an angel of light. It is probable, therefore, as Hodge comments, 'that the statement rests on the general doctrine of the Bible concerning the great adversary. He is everywhere represented as the deceiver, assuming false guises, and making false representations'. And, as Hodge goes on truly to remind us, 'Satan does not come to us as Satan; neither does sin present itself to us as sin, but in the guise of virtue; and the teachers of error set themselves forth as the special advocates of truth'.

15. Christ has His *ministers*, and so has Satan; and, just as Christ's ministers have something of the sense of vocation and mission which characterized Him who was sent by the Father into the world to perform His gracious work of redemption, so Satan's ministers exhibit the nature and methods of him by whom they are diabolically inspired, and whose kingdom of darkness they are engaged in extending. It is *no great thing*, the apostle remarks, if Satan's power to present himself in a guise foreign to his real nature should also be found in those enlisted in his service. Appearing as *the ministers of righteousness*, i.e. eloquent advocates of the Pharisaic doctrine that men can put themselves right with God by their own unaided efforts, they are in fact deceivers of others because they are themselves deceived. Evil does not become good by being called good, and ministers of Satan do not cease to be such by parading as advocates of righteousness. At the moment, such men may seem to be successful; but in the end they will be shown up in their true colours and receive such punishment as befits their deeds. It is an axiom of biblical Christianity that, however much the wicked may seem at present to flourish, their *end shall be according to their works*. The statement of Pr. xxiv. 12, 'Shall not he render to every man according to his works?', is quoted by Paul in Rom. ii. 6 as a description of God's activity on the final day of wrath, and again in 2 Tim. iv. 14 with reference to the punishment that awaits Alexander the coppersmith who had done him much wrong. It is also echoed in Gal. v. 10 when he states that the troubler of the Galatians, whoever he is, will 'bear his judgment'; and in 1 Pet. i. 17 where God is said without respect of persons to judge 'according to every man's work'. The divine recompense will become effective, as Jesus said, when 'the Son of man shall come in the glory of his Father with his angels; and then he shall reward every man according to his works' (Mt. xvi. 27).

It is a mark of the shallowness of much of the religious

thinking in the modern world that Menzies, writing in 1912, should feel it necessary to describe verses 13–15 as 'one of the hastiest utterances in Paul's writings', and to add that 'many of the best friends of the apostle do not defend his controversial style in this passage'. It is possible to value toleration so much that clear-cut distinctions between right and wrong become impossible. The New Testament writers are hampered by no such inhibitions! Jesus again and again denounced the Pharisees as 'hypocrites'; and He told the disbelieving Jews at Jerusalem that they were 'of their father the devil' and were exhibiting the murderous characteristics of their sire (see Jn. viii. 44). False religious teachers are everywhere stated to be what, in fact, they really are; and perversions of Christianity are never presented as though they were partial understandings of truth, but denounced as destructive of truth. The Christian is warned against passing final judgment upon anyone, however evil he may be seen to be; but he is taught to refrain from all who 'having a form of godliness, deny the power thereof' (see 2 Tim. iii. 1–5); and severe woes are pronounced by Isaiah against those 'that call evil good, and good evil; that put darkness for light, and light for darkness' (Is. v. 20). So far then from being 'unwilling to defend' Paul's statements in these verses, we ought rather to learn from them to call evil by its proper name, and never to compromise with those who present it to us as something different from what it really is.

It is recorded by Irenaeus that Polycarp, the saintly bishop of Smyrna, when accosted by the heretic Marcion with the question 'Do you recognize me?', replied, 'I recognize you as the first-born of Satan.' And Irenaeus adds, 'So great was the fear of the apostles and their disciples lest they should speak a single word of fellowship to those who adulterated the truth.'

g. Paul's credentials and experiences (xi. 16–33)

16. After painting his opponents in their true colours, Paul returns to the subject of 'boasting' begun in the earlier part of the chapter. He repeats that all boasting is foolish, and he would not be counted *a fool* by any man. It goes entirely against the grain with him to have to defend himself against his detractors with words which sound the jarring note of self-praise. Not all the Corinthians, however, are so appreciative of their apostle that they would consider it a mark of wisdom on his part if he refrained from saying anything which might appear to be boastful; and it is to this wavering minority that he now appeals to grant to himself the same privilege they so readily allow to others, who are only too eager to 'talk big' about their qualifications and their achievements. The reference to these 'others' is missed in AV by the failure to translate the word meaning 'also' (inserted in RV) before *may boast*.

17, 18. These two verses are rightly regarded in RSV as parenthetical, for the particle *for* in verse 19 introduces a sentence giving a reason why the Corinthians should readily do what the apostle has asked them to do in verse 16. The point stressed in that verse is now elaborated further. To speak in *this confidence of boasting* (RSV 'in this boastful confidence') is to speak foolishly because it is to speak *not after the Lord*. It is not how Christ Himself spoke; for, though no one ever made higher claims for Himself than He did, He was not speaking as a mere man assuming an equality with God to which He had no right, as His opponents thought when they accused Him of glorifying Himself. And because Christ never spoke boastfully, His Spirit never leads His disciples to do so. No boasting could ever be said to be a fruit of the Spirit! But there were occasions, such as this present one, when it had a negative part to play in clearing away misconceptions which had arisen in the minds of some of Paul's weaker converts, and in helping them to recover their grip upon the truth they had already received. When his own efforts were being depreciated, and there was a danger in consequence that the gospel, which could never be dissociated in the converts' minds from him who had proclaimed it to them, might also be discredited, then the apostle felt it a duty to indulge in this disagreeable task. Hence, he does not hesitate to say, *Seeing that many glory after the flesh, I will glory also.*

It is clear from verse 22 that by glorying *after the flesh* is meant boasting about external advantages and privileges, such as nationality, birth and position, which were not due to any merit whatever on the part of the persons concerned; and it is also clear from the context that Paul is going to meet his opponents on their own ground, and that the word *also* must be taken to imply 'after the flesh, as they do'. It is not, however, clear whether by *many* the apostle is speaking generally, drawing attention to a common habit, or with a more limited reference to the situation at Corinth. If the latter, then the number of the false apostles would appear to have been considerable.

19. Paul here justifies, with no little irony, the appeal to the Corinthians made in verse 16 to allow him to boast as a fool, on the ground that they are people who *are wise*, some of them so wise that they can tolerate even *fools gladly*, and, therefore, they could not possibly have any objection to what he was doing.

20. But not only do some of the Corinthians gladly put up with the folly that proceeded from the mouths of these bombastic talkers; they are also content to suffer personal indignities at their hands such as their own apostle could never dream of inflicting upon them. Paul's opponents were not only braggarts, but tyrants, determined to enslave their victims. The verb translated *bring into bondage, katadoulō*, is used in Gal. ii. 4 (and nowhere else in the New Testament) of the Judaizers who were trying to enslave the Galatians by making them keep the Jewish law in its entirety; and it may be that it has the same implication here. Many commentators, however, consider that the verb, though active in form, has in effect a middle sense. These tyrants are endeavouring to enslave the Corinthians *to themselves*, so that in *all* things they may be the servants of their will.

In their greed they use every available means of extracting money from those who come under their power. They *devour* (RSV 'preys upon') them, the same verb *katesthiō* being used here as in our Lord's denunciation of the Pharisees because they 'devoured widows' houses' (see Lk. xx. 47).

By inserting the words *of you* after *take* AV gives the verb *lambanō* the sense, which it is capable of bearing, of 'get something out of you'; but this is a weaker charge to bring against the tyrants than that set forth in the previous verb *devour*. The RV and RSV renderings 'taketh you captive' and 'takes advantage of you' are, therefore, preferable. The verb seems to suggest here, as Plummer points out, that these unscrupulous rogues are trying to 'catch' the Corinthians 'as birds in a snare, or fishes with bait' (cf. the use of the same verb in Lk. v. 5).

By *exalt himself* (RSV 'puts on airs') something more is implied than the 'boasting' to which reference has already been made. The meaning of the verb here used *epairetai* is brought out better by Plummer in his translation 'lords it over you'.

To *smite on the face* or mouth is a mark of the greatest disrespect. It was an indignity suffered literally by Micaiah at the hands of the false prophet Zedekiah (1 Ki. xxii. 24), by Jesus at the hands of those who arrested Him (Lk. xxii. 64, AV), and by Paul at the instigation of the high priest Ananias (Acts xxiii. 2). Some commentators take the expression here also in the literal sense, and infer that physical violence was used on the Corinthians; others, with perhaps greater probability, follow Chrysostom in regarding it as symbolic of any kind of humiliating treatment.

21. This is a difficult verse, as it is not clear whether Paul is reproaching himself, or the Corinthians, or both. The Greek means simply 'I speak by way of reproach'. Some commentators have held that the object of *I speak* is all that Paul has just been saying about the indignities the Corinthians are prepared to suffer at the hands of their would-be tyrants, and that the apostle is now stating that he has been drawing attention to this subject so as to put the Corinthians to shame. The difficulty of this exegesis is that, if it is adopted, the last clause in the first sentence does not appear to have much meaning. We should have to suppose that *as though*, *hōs hoti*, is in fact causal, and that Paul is saying that he is mentioning this matter now because he had been too weak to do so when he was last present at Corinth—an admission of failure indeed, which scarcely does justice to the qualifying *hōs* ('as if'). More probable then is the view that *I speak* governs the clause *as though we had been weak*, and that Paul is reproaching himself, though in irony, for having been weak in comparison with the bullies who have shown such strength. This is the interpretation of RSV 'To my shame, I must say, we were too weak for that!' Menzies gives a similar explanation, though he eliminates the irony, and supposes that Paul's words imply that the Corinthians as well as himself deserve reproach. 'It is not a creditable thing he has to speak of; yet he must say it, he has come short in firmness and in show of authority . . . but the discredit is for the Corinthians too that they should prefer those who bully them to one who treated them gently and insisted so little on his rights and dignity.'

The last sentence in this verse is an assertion that, whatever weakness Paul may or may not have shown, he is bold enough now, though it means speaking foolishly, to counter-attack his opponents on every charge they bring against him.

22. It is clear from this verse that Paul's opponents boasted a great deal about their descent. They were proud to speak the language of the people who in the distant past had come from beyond the great river Euphrates, the word *Hebrew* having as its root meaning 'beyond'. In Acts vi. 1, it is used to distinguish Hebrew- or Aramaic-speaking Jewish Christians from those who spoke Greek. In this matter of descent, however, his opponents were in no way superior to Paul; for though born in Tarsus in Cilicia he was a Hebrew and of Hebrew stock (see Phil. iii. 5). He could study the Scriptures in the language in which they were written; and he was able to speak the Aramaic dialect so well that he could hold the attention of an ill-disposed rabble at Jerusalem when he addressed them from the steps leading up from the Temple to the fortress Antonia (see Acts xxi. 40, xxii. 2).

The false apostles were also proud to be *Israelites*. It was indeed a title of privilege, a daily reminder that they belonged to the people adopted by God to be His own peculiar possession, the special object of His care, the guardians of His law, and chosen to reflect His glory to the world (see Rom. ix. 4). As *Israelites* they were descended from Jacob, who received the name Israel when he had proved himself to be no longer the 'supplanter' but a man who persevered with God (see Gn. xxxii. 28 and cf. Jn. i. 47). But even more than this could be claimed by Paul's opponents. They were *the seed of Abraham*, to whom the promises concerning the blessings that his descendants would one day enjoy had been made. But, in all this, Paul's opponents were in no way superior to himself. He too could claim to be an Israelite, not merely by reason of his birth, but because even after his new birth as a Christian he had not forfeited his right to the title. Now that the seed of Abraham had come in the Person of Jesus the Christ, all believers in Him were members of the true Israel of God, heirs to the promises made to the patriarchs, promises to which no restrictive conditions had been attached such as compulsory circumcision or a readiness to observe the entire Jewish law (see Gal. iii. 16, 17).

23. Paul's opponents also asserted that they were *ministers* of Christ. In this verse, he neither defends nor denies their claim. He merely affirms that if they do make this a ground for boasting, he himself can put forward a counter-claim to be far superior to them in this matter. To make such an affirmation means to speak *as a fool*, for, in Plummer's words, 'to glory about so sacred a matter as the service of Christ is downright madness'. The word here translated *fool*, *paraphronōn*, is probably a stronger word than *aphrōn* similarly translated in verses 16 and 19. So far as they can be distinguished the former describes someone who is 'out of his senses' while the latter suggests a person 'lacking in sense'.

The translation *I am more* might imply that Paul is more than a minister of Christ. The true meaning is that he is more a minister of Christ than his opponents. This is brought out in RV, 'I more' (there is no *am* in the original) and in RSV, 'I am a better one'. Paul claims superiority over his opponents as 'a minister of Christ' on four points: (1) He has undertaken more numerous and more arduous evangelistic campaigns than they (for this is the probable meaning of *in labours more abundant*). (2) He has been the victim, as they have not, of excessive corporal punishment (the word *huperballontōs*, Vulg. *super modum*, would appear to be better translated *above measure*, i.e. above normal or reasonable measure, than by RSV 'count-less'). (3) He had been more frequently *in prisons* than they. We have definite information of only one imprisonment of Paul previous to the writing of this Epistle, viz. at Philippi (see Acts xvi). Clement of Rome, however, writing in AD 96, states that Paul was imprisoned seven times; and it is usually supposed by modern scholars that Paul was in prison at Ephesus during the stay recorded in Acts xix, the main evidence being the existence of the ruins of a tower there known in tradition as 'Paul's prison'. Indirect evidence for this incarceration may perhaps be found in 2 Cor. i. 8-10. (4) So constantly is he in immediate danger of death that he can say 'I die daily' (1 Cor. xv. 31). He would appear to have been face to face with death quite recently at Ephesus (see 2 Cor. i. 9).

24, 25. Specific examples are now given in confirmation of the statements of the previous verse. Up to the time of writing Paul had been chastised eight times; and it is a reasonable inference from the context that some of these beatings were so severe that he nearly died under them. Five times he had received, at the hands of his fellow countrymen, the maximum penalty that the Jewish law allowed a judge to order when a guilty man deserved to be beaten (see Dt. xxv. 1-3). The law stipulated 'Forty stripes he may give him, he shall not exceed'; and, in order that this precept might be punctiliously observed, it was later ordained that thirty-nine stripes only should be inflicted. As the lash or scourge contained three thongs, this meant that thirteen strokes were given. This terrible punishment was adumbrated in the warning given by Jesus to His disciples 'they will scourge you in their synagogues' (Mt. x. 17). Chastisement *with rods* was suffered by Paul during his stay in the Roman colony of Philippi. It was illegal for a Roman citizen, such as Paul, to be sentenced to this punishment, but it would seem that brutal local magistrates often disregarded this privilege, particularly when the populace was putting pressure upon them. This sentence was carried out by the lictors or rod-bearers, who attended upon the two praetors who were the executive officials in a Roman colony. There is no mention in Acts of the other two occasions when Paul was beaten in this way. Rendall points out that they must have been either at Roman colonies or in places that came under proconsular jurisdiction, and that the choice would seem to be limited to Pisidian Antioch or Lystra (cf. 2 Tim. iii. 11).

There is no record in Acts that Paul *suffered shipwreck* previous to the final voyage to Rome. Rendall's attempts to locate and date the three occasions referred to by Paul seem vitiated by the assumption that shipwrecks could only take place at certain times of the year. But, as Menzies remarks, 'In the coasting voyages of the Mediterranean at that time shipwreck was always very possible'.

Paul was *stoned* at Lystra, when his friends believed him to be dead (see Acts xiv. 19). At Iconium a threat to stone him was not carried out, as the apostles were able to escape in time (see Acts xiv. 5, 6).

The translation of *pepoiēka en buthō* by *I have been in the deep* is obviously misleading, as Paul did not spend twenty-four hours under water! The meaning is brought out in RSV 'adrift at sea', i.e. clinging to a raft in the open sea. The use here of the perfect tense, as distinct from the previous aorists, does not necessarily imply that this last experience was so recent as to be still very vivid in the apostle's memory, for in New Testament Greek the perfect often has the force of an aorist.

26. The phrase *in journeyings often* is introductory to what follows; for Paul specifies the various dangers that had to be faced by anyone who had to make frequent journeys in the Mediterranean world of the first century. His own particular journeys were rendered still more hazardous because he was subjected to the hatred of all men, to whatever region of the world he might go for Christ's sake (see Mt. x. 22).

For *waters* we should read with RV 'rivers', often swollen by floods and difficult to ford as bridges were few. The dangers from *robbers* or brigands are illustrated in our Lord's parable of the Good Samaritan. Dangers experienced by Paul from his *own countrymen* are to be found *passim* in Acts. Their hatred of Paul was due to his acceptance of a crucified Messiah and to his abandonment of the Pharisaic doctrine of justification by works of law; and their jealousy of him was stimulated by the success he had achieved in obtaining converts from the Gentile God-fearers whom they had attracted to their synagogues in the hope that they would become proselytes. *Perils by the heathen* were encountered when Paul was brought before Roman tribunals, as at Philippi and Ephesus. *Perils in the city* had to be faced every time the mob became incensed against him, as had recently happened at Ephesus. The mention of *perils in the wilderness*, due to storms in exposed places and perhaps to wild beasts lurking in the vicinity, is evidence that Paul was not always able to keep to the well-frequented highways on his missions, and that many of his journeys off the main roads have not been recorded in Acts. *Perils of the sea* were not absent for long, even when conditions were comparatively speaking favourable. And most treacherous of all were the *perils* due to *false brethren*. There has never been a time in the history of the Christian Church when it was free from treachery within. There was a Judas among the original apostles, and there have been traitors in the camp ever since. Menzies notices that Paul makes no mention of perils due to snow, as he seems to have avoided winter travel, nor of the perils of wayside inns!

27. 'This verse', as Menzies suggests, 'seems to refer not to hardship of travel, but to Paul's life when he was in a town

working at one of his churches.' Certainly the words translated
in weariness and painfulness (RSV 'toil and hardship') suggests a
reference to Paul's manual labour. The former, *kopos*, denotes
the fatigue, and the latter, *mochthos*, the hardship of prolonged
manual toil.

Watchings is more probably a reference to sleepless nights
due to anxiety or physical discomfort, than to voluntary vigils
undertaken for the purpose of work or prayer. Similarly,
fastings should be construed in close connection with *hunger
and thirst* as physical hardships laid upon the apostle by force
of circumstance, rather than voluntary fasts submitted to for
religious ends. There is no evidence that Paul ever fasted in the
latter sense after his missionary work had begun. He may,
however, have been among those in the church at Antioch
who fasted before the decision was made that he and Barnabas
should undertake a mission to the Gentiles (see Acts xiii. 3).
Cold and nakedness (RSV 'exposure') completes the picture of the
apostle's discomforts while toiling for his living in 'reduced'
circumstances. 'The details recorded in verses 23–27', comments Strachan, 'indicate how many experiences of this kind
in Paul's life are unrecorded—indeed had none to record them,
for he must often have suffered alone. Here he wears his pains
like decorations.'

28. The translation *those things that are without* is due to the
influence of Vulg. *extrinsecus*. However, the Greek, *tōn parektos*,
can scarcely mean anything except 'the things not mentioned'; so RSV 'apart from other things'. As Plummer points
out, 'the idea of *exception* rather than that of *externality* domi-
nates the word *parektos*'. It is used as a preposition in the much-
discussed *exception* clause in the teaching on divorce in Mt. v.
32. The sense then is not that Paul, having listed some of the
outward perils of his life, now passes on to his more inward
trials. Rather does he now mention, according to the most
probable interpretation of this verse, a perpetual anxiety from
which he is never free for a single day, *the care of all the churches.*
That which cometh upon me translates the reading of the later

MSS, *hē episustasis mou*, and the second clause *the care of all the churches* is taken as explanatory of it. RV translates the older and better attested reading, *hē epistasis moi*, 'that which presseth upon me', but also regards the second clause as explanatory. Paul is daily burdened by the moral and doctrinal problems referred to him by the churches, which look to him as their apostle, and by their call to him to settle personal disputes and reunite opposing factions.

In spite of the stronger external evidence for the RV reading Field[1] argues that it is difficult to find any parallel for this rare word meaning what the RV assumes it to mean. Normally *epistasis* seems to mean 'close attention'; so Alford here translates 'my care day by day, my anxiety for all the churches', which gives a weak tautologous sense; and the word cannot have that meaning in Acts xxiv. 12, the only other place where it is found in the New Testament. *Episustasis* is used in Nu. xvi. 40, of the hostile combination formed by Korah and his company against Moses. Field believes that this is the true meaning here. 'The Apostle is describing two distinct elements of the harassing and wearing life which he led; *first*, the "caballing" or "conspiring against him" of those rulers or members of the church with whom he was in daily communication; and *secondly*, the interest which, from his position, he was led to take in the concerns of distant churches. Without some allusion to the former of these, no description of his apostolical labours and sufferings would have been complete.' Chrysostom, also reading *episustasis*, interpreted it, in a wider sense than that advocated by Field, of the tribulations and disturbances which crowded in upon the apostle day by day. But, as the MSS evidence so strongly favours *epistasis*, and there is no connecting particle *and* between the two clauses, it would seem that the English versions are right in regarding the second as explanatory of the first, and that the probable sense is given in RSV, 'the daily pressure upon me of my anxiety for all the churches'.

[1] F. Field, *Notes on the Translation of the New Testament*, pp. 185, 186 (C.U.P., 1899).

29. The care of all the churches made great and continual demands upon the apostle's charity, for their multifarious problems could not be solved except in the spirit of Christian love. In this verse, Paul draws attention to the two complementary aspects of that love, which by the grace of God he is able to exhibit. These are sympathy with the weak, and indignation at the perpetration of moral wrong. By the *weak* he means all who feel themselves to be slighted or wronged, or who have unduly sensitive consciences and moral scruples (cf. Rom. xiv. 1; 1 Cor. ix. 22). Paul, strong in faith himself, feels the 'weakness' of all such as though it was his own. In no unreal sense he suffers with them.

While all Christians would agree that sympathy is of the essence of Christian love, it is not so generally recognized that without moral indignation that love is imperfect. We need to remember that the meek and gentle Jesus (see x. 1) was filled with burning indignation when He saw stumbling-blocks placed in the way of the weak, little ones caused to sin (see Mt. xviii. 6, RSV), and burdens laid upon their fellow-men by those who ought to have been their helpers. No one can read such a chapter as Mt. xxiii without feeling the white-hot resentment of the Master at all that is false, hypocritical, and cruel. Similarly, when Paul saw charlatans diverting the unwary in his churches from the pathway of true religion, or heard of moral offences committed by the Christians themselves such as were frowned upon even in pagan society, his love glowed with righteous wrath. It was 'terrible as an army with banners', as it went forth to champion the cause of the weak and the oppressed. No better illustrations of the apostle's question, *Who is offended, and I burn not?* (Moffatt, 'Whose faith is hurt, and I am not aglow with indignation?') could be found than the Epistle to the Galatians and these closing chapters of 2 Corinthians.[1]

30. Some commentators regard *I will glory* as a strict future; and, beginning a new paragraph at this point, they

[1] For some excellent remarks on moral indignation see James Moffatt, *Love in the New Testament*, pp. 30–32 (Hodder and Stoughton, 1929).

assume that the reference is to what follows. But it is more probable that Paul is stating in general terms the paradoxical truth which has emerged since he began 'boasting' about himself. He had set out to counter the claims put forward by the arrogant false apostles, but he has, in fact, been laying stress upon the very things about which the naturally boastful person would say nothing—his humiliations and his sufferings! What might be called a 'principle of boasting' seems to have been formulating itself. I will glory, he says, if I must, but only *of the things which concern mine infirmities.*

31. This amazing record of his afflictions as an apostle of Christ might appear to those hearing it for the first time incredulous. The apostle, therefore, now calls God to witness that everything he has said bears the hall-mark of truth. There has been no inaccuracy and no over-statement. Other similar solemn assertions by Paul of the truth of what he is saying are found in Gal. i. 20, Rom. ix. 1, and 1 Tim. ii. 7. For the significance of the expression *The God and Father of our Lord Jesus Christ* see the note on i. 3. *Christ* is omitted in RV, as it is not found here in P. 46, Aleph, B, and other ancient authorities.

32, 33. As verse 31 seems to mark the conclusion of a section, it is at first sight a little strange to find, in these verses, a further detailed illustration of the infirmities summarized earlier in the chapter. It may be that Paul, after taking what is virtually an oath in the previous verse, remembers the remarkable incident at the outset of his Christian ministry which he perhaps felt was not fully covered by the previous classification of his sufferings. It is possible that his enemies had spread a rumour that he had acted as a coward in escaping so ignominiously from Damascus. The truth was, he here implies, that the hatred of the Jews, even when reinforced by the armed might of a powerful ruler, could not thwart the purposes of God, who used this very humiliating but effective means of setting His servant forward along the road of service ordained for him.

Aretas was a title for Arabian kings similar to that of Pharaoh used in Egypt. This particular monarch ruled over

Nabataea, between the Red Sea and the Euphrates, from 9 BC to AD 40. He was thus reigning when Herod Antipas, the tetrarch of Galilee in the ministry of Jesus, divorced his daughter in order to marry Herodias, wife of his own half-brother Philip. The nature of the position of Aretas' *governor* (Gk. *ethnarchēs*) at Damascus is uncertain. F. F. Bruce[1] inclines to the view that 'he was Aretas's representative in Damascus, who looked after the interests of the many Nabataean subjects in the city while it was under Roman rule'. We are able to combine the information contained in these verses with what is said in Acts ix. 24, 25 if we suppose that the Jews at Damascus enlisted the services of the 'ethnarch' in their determined effort to get Paul out of the city. In Acts ix. 24 we read, 'they (i.e. the Jews) watched the gates day and night to kill him'. In this passage, Paul asserts that *the governor under Aretas . . . kept the city . . . with a garrison, desirous to apprehend me* (RV omits *desirous*, which is not found in B, D and the Latin versions, and renders 'in order to take me'). There is no contradiction between Luke and Paul, as it is probable that the Jews urged the governor to take this action. The Greek verb *phroureō* is translated in AV *kept the city with a garrison*, and in RV 'guarded the city'. Both translations are possible, as the word was used for watching a city either from outside or from within.[2] On the assumption that the 'ethnarch' had jurisdiction *within* the city, Paul's narrative can be most easily harmonized with Acts ix. 24, by translating the verb 'placed a watch at the gates'. In other words, the wording in Acts does not necessarily imply that the Jews were *themselves* watching the gates; they had in fact urged the ethnarch to see that they were guarded so as to prevent Paul's escape. To Luke the Jews were the 'villains of the piece'. In two of the other passages in the New Testament where the same verb is found, it is used metaphorically of God's protection of His people (see 1 Pet. i. 5 and Phil. iv. 7); He keeps ward over them as a garrison keeps ward over a town.

[1] See *The Acts of the Apostles*, p. 205 (Tyndale Press, 1951).
[2] See F. Field, *op. cit.*, pp. 186, 187.

The details of the dramatic escape of Paul from Damascus are clearer here than in Acts ix. 25, where there is no mention of *through a window* (Gk. *thuris*, 'little door'), an aperture in the city wall. *By the wall* translates the Greek *dia tou teichous*, which is an idiomatic expression equivalent to '*via* the wall'. RSV connects the expression with 'through a window' and translates it 'in the wall'; but, though the window *was* in the wall, this is not an accurate translation of the original.

Paul could never forget this experience, harbinger as it was of so much that was to follow. As Calvin well remarks, 'this persecution was his first apprenticeship'. He was initiated on this memorable occasion into the many things that he had to suffer for his Master's sake (see Acts ix. 16).

h. Paul's visions and thorn in the flesh (xii. 1–10)

1. There is considerable textual variation in this verse. In the text underlying AV, *It is not expedient* is the principal verb in the first sentence and governs *to glory*; *doubtless* translates the particle *dē*; and the second sentence is introduced by the particle *gar*, 'for'. The failure to translate this latter particle renders the AV somewhat obscure. If this text, found in the later MSS, is followed, the meaning will be, in Hodge's words, 'Boasting is not expedient (therefore I desist) for I will now pass to something else'. This sense does not, however, suit the context, for it would seem that Paul's opponents were boasting about their visions, and Paul now counter-attacks them on their own ground just as he has done in the previous chapter. We should, therefore, certainly follow the text found in the most ancient authorities. In this, *dei* takes the place of *dē* giving the meaning 'I must glory', a sentence complete in itself; and instead of *it is not expedient* an expression is found meaning 'while it is not expedient', which stands in contrast with the following clause introduced not by 'for', but by a particle meaning 'but'. The full sense of *this* text is well brought out in RSV, 'I must boast; there is nothing to be gained by it, but I will go on to visions and revelations of the Lord'.

The genitive *of the Lord* is subjective, not objective. The vision which Paul is about to mention was not one in which he saw the heavenly Christ, but one which the heavenly Christ enabled him to see.

The difference between *visions, optasiai,* and *revelations, apokalupseis,* is that in the former something is visually presented to the observer, while 'revelations' are not always mediated through what can be seen. Most visions, however, contain a revelation.

2. Paul confines himself in this 'boasting' about visions to a single experience enjoyed *fourteen years ago.* The date is specific, for the word *above* has no textual authority, and would seem to have been inserted by AV because this experience was mistakenly assumed to be the conversion experience on the road to Damascus. But the latter took place more than twenty years before the writing of this Epistle; it was, moreover, something to which Paul was never tired of drawing attention, for on it rested his entire claim to be an apostle of Jesus Christ. The somewhat enigmatic reference to himself as *a man in Christ* is due partly to his reluctance to speak about the subject, and partly to a desire to give the impression that *any* Christian (for a Christian cannot better be described than as 'a man in Christ') might have been privileged to experience this vision, while he alone could have experienced the special vision which was the means of his conversion. AV, both here and in verse 3, wrongly renders 'I know' as *I knew,* thereby giving the impression that the man in question was no longer known to Paul!

In this vision the apostle was translated out of this world of time and space, though, whether his soul was for the time being detached from his body, or whether both soul and body made the celestial journey, he *cannot tell.* The literal meaning of this last phrase is 'I do not know', the word 'know' signifying 'remember' as in 1 Cor. i. 16.[1] The vision was entirely God's doing; and *God knoweth,* and no one else, how the transference from earth to heaven was effected.

Caught up accentuates the truth that Paul himself, though he

[1] See F. Field, *op. cit.,* p. 187.

was conscious of what was happening, remained entirely passive during the vision, which was in no way self-induced. The same verb is found in Acts viii. 39, where it is stated that 'the Spirit of the Lord caught away Philip', who after being supernaturally guided was found later at Azotus. It is also used in 1 Thes. iv. 17 in Paul's description of the Parousia, 'we which are alive and remain shall be caught up . . . to meet the Lord in the air'.

The expression *the third heaven* is found only here in the New Testament, though in Eph. iv. 10 (RV) we read, 'all the heavens'. In later Jewish writings, both before and after the time of Christ, the conception of seven heavens is found.[1] But for Paul to speak of a *third* heaven, with the implication that there were four other and higher heavens, would be out of keeping with the present context where he seems to be emphasizing the supreme blessedness of the state into which he had been caught up. As Plummer, following Calvin, well comments: 'He is using language which was to be understood by the Corinthians, and it is not likely that he expected them to know about seven heavens: whereas "even to the third heaven" might convey to anyone the idea of the most sublime condition conceivable.'

3, 4. It would seem that *paradise* is virtually a synonym for *the third heaven*, but that it is specifically mentioned by Paul because in some later Jewish books (e.g. *The Secrets of Enoch*[2]) the third heaven was pictured as containing an abode for the wicked as well as an abode for the blessed. This latter dwelling-place is designated 'paradise', a Persian word meaning 'park', which is used in LXX of the garden of Eden, and in the New Testament for the place where the glory lost in Eden is regained by the faithful. The penitent thief was promised direct access to this blessed abode on the day of his death and in company with his newly accepted Lord (see Lk. xxiii. 43);

---

[1] Cf. *The Testaments of the Twelve Patriarchs*, 'Testament of Levi', chapter iii.

[2] The text of this work can be found in R. H. Charles, *Apocrypha and Pseudepigrapha of the Old Testament*, Vol. II.

and in Rev. ii. 7, those who 'overcome' during their earthly pilgrimage are promised immortality portrayed under the imagery of 'the tree of life, which is in the midst of the paradise of God'.

Paul says nothing at all about what he *saw* during his rapturous experience in paradise. What he *heard* he describes as *unspeakable words, which it is not lawful for a man to utter*. It is clear that this particular revelation was for Paul alone, to strengthen his belief in the reality of heaven and to reassure him during his sufferings on earth of the glory that awaited him for remaining faithful to his Lord. The date of the vision *fourteen years ago* is evidence that Paul was granted this encouraging experience a year or two before embarking upon his great Gentile missions. The New Testament is deliberately reticent about the details of the after-life; and it becomes Christians to refrain from idle and curious speculation on the subject. The things that are necessary for our salvation God has made plain; what has not been made plain is not necessary. As Hodge well says: 'The communications made to the apostle he was not allowed to make known to others. The veil which conceals the mysteries and glories of heaven God has not permitted to be raised. It is enough that we know that in that world the saints shall be made perfectly holy and perfectly blessed in the full enjoyment of God for ever.' Nowhere in the New Testament is heaven described; but in the poetical imagery of the Revelation of John are to be found flashes of its glory sufficient to stimulate the imagination of the saints, to encourage them in their sufferings upon earth, and to intensify their longing for their permanent home.

5. Though this vision was a fact and no delusion, and though Paul could glory in it without any vanity because it was God's doing and not his, nevertheless he does not wish anyone to suppose that he is adding to his own personal reputation by relating it. So he again speaks of the recipient of the vision as though he were someone other than himself, and adds that *of myself*, i.e. with reference to himself, he will abide by 'the principle of boasting' he has been led to adopt it, i.e. *I will not glory, but in mine infirmities*.

6. But the apostle does not wish to give the impression that he has not good grounds for glorying; so, for the benefit of his detractors, he adds that, even though he should *desire to glory* (about the things which were not 'unspeakable'), he would not be speaking as *a fool*, bragging about what had no substance in it, for all that he would be saying would be *the truth*. But he refrains from speaking this whole truth, for many of his spiritual experiences are of such a nature that they could not be verified by other people. He would have his converts judge him solely by what they saw him to be, and by what they heard him say when he preached the gospel to them or wrote to them in his letters. *Of me* is misleading, as the original does not mean 'about me' but 'from me'.

7. The reading underlying the text of AV in this verse now has the additional support of P. 46, and is preferable to that found in Aleph and B which underlies RV. The word 'wherefore' found in RV was probably inserted when the words *through the abundance of the revelations* were construed with the previous verse. With either reading, however, the general sense is much the same. The apostle is, in fact, saying that, while there may be a danger lest others should think more highly of him than they ought to think because of the visions and revelations he enjoys, there is no danger that he himself will. God has taken effective steps to prevent that by giving him *a thorn in the flesh*. This difficult expression, *skolops tē sarki*, has given rise to an immense amount of discussion and to a great variety of interpretations, none of which has received anything approaching general acceptance.

There would seem to be a growing consensus of opinion among scholars that the right translation of *skolops* is *thorn* and not 'stake' as RV mg. For although the word, originally denoting something pointed, had as its primary meaning in classical Greek 'pale' or 'stake', it was also used for 'thorn'; and this use predominates in LXX (cf. Nu. xxxiii. 55; Ezk.

xxviii. 24; and Ho. ii. 6). The examples of the word in the papyri (see M & M) also strongly support this rendering. The meaning of *tē sarki* is not so certain. The dative case could either be locative, *in the flesh*, or a *dativus incommodi*, 'for the inconvenience of the flesh'. If 'a thorn *in* the flesh' is the right translation, 'flesh' would seem to denote physical flesh; and the 'thorn' would most naturally be something embedded in it, and, therefore, something malignant, for thorns embedded in the flesh tend to fester. It must, however, be confessed that it would have been more natural for the apostle to have inserted the preposition 'in' before 'the flesh', if this had been the implication (cf. Nu. xxxiii. 55, LXX). On the other hand, if the translation '*for* the flesh' is adopted, then it becomes possible, and indeed more natural, to understand 'flesh' in its peculiarly Pauline sense of 'the lower nature' which still remains active even in the regenerate; and by 'thorn' could be meant painful experiences which pierce this nature from without and prevent it from becoming aggressive.

Those who take 'flesh' to mean 'physical flesh' usually interpret the 'thorn' in the light of Gal. iv. 13–15; they assume that Paul is speaking of some physical malady, either inherent in his body which became active from time to time, perhaps especially after he had experienced a vision, or some external infection to which he was a ready victim. When the interpretation of the present verse is tied up in this way with the Galatians passage, it becomes natural to narrow down the reference to some ailment which helps to explain the colourful language there used by the apostle. Thus, from Paul's statement that the Galatians would have 'plucked out their eyes' and given them to him if that had been possible, some have assumed that he suffered from bad eye-sight. Others, from his remark that it was because of an infirmity of the flesh that he preached the gospel to them on his first visit (see iv. 13, RV), have drawn two conclusions: first, that it was an attack of malaria fever contracted in the low-lying district of Pamphylia which led the apostle to journey north into Pisidia within the Roman province of Galatia; and, secondly, that this was an illness to which Paul was particularly prone. The reference, moreover, to the charity displayed by the Galatians in not despising or rejecting (the last word meaning literally 'spitting out') what was a temptation to them in Paul's flesh, has led others to the view that the 'thorn' is a symbolic description of epilepsy, which was sometimes called *morbus qui sputatur*, 'the disease which is spat at'. There is, however, no real reason why the reference in Gal. iv should be considered in connection with this present verse in 2 Corinthians. In Gal. iv. 13 Paul speaks of '*an* infirmity of the flesh'. There is no definite article, and there is no personal pronoun; he is not, in other words, referring to 'that constantly recurring trouble of mine which elsewhere I call my thorn in the flesh'. It may well have been a rather exceptional illness which had caused him to journey into Galatia at that particular time.

It must be acknowledged that the general impression of Paul that the reader obtains from his Epistles, not least from 2 Corinthians, and from Acts, is of a man with an exceptionally strong constitution and remarkable powers of physical endurance. This is not really compatible with the view that he was the constant victim of a severe physical ailment.

It may well be then that the interpretation of 'the thorn in the flesh' as a physical malady, which has been the view most popular with modern Protestants, should be abandoned in favour of the exegesis of the Reformers and many of the early Fathers that the 'thorn' was *spiritual* in character, sent by God '*for* the flesh', i.e. to prick the bubble of the apostle's arrogance, traces of which almost certainly lingered on even after he had been converted from Pharisaism. It was liable perhaps to be aggravated by a feeling of spiritual superiority engendered by his visions.

Chrysostom's exegesis is that there were times when God would not permit Paul's preaching to progress, in order to check the high thoughts of the apostle, but allowed his adversaries to maltreat him. He interpreted the *messenger of Satan* personally, as a reference to Alexander the coppersmith (2 Tim. iv. 14), the party of Hymenaeus and Philetus (2 Tim. ii.

17), and all the adversaries of the Word, who were doing Satan's business.

Tyndale would seem to have been unduly influenced by the Vulgate in his translation, 'unquietness of the flesh'; for the Latin version, *stimulus carnis*, had been almost invariably understood in the middle ages to refer to the lustful thoughts to which monks in their seclusion were especially prone. Calvin and Luther rightly rejected this interpretation, for 'flesh' in the Pauline Epistles cannot be confined to the sphere of sex, as it tends to be today when we speak of 'sins of the flesh' (see Gal. v. 19–21). Calvin thought that 'the thorn in the flesh' included every temptation by which Paul was assailed, 'the flesh' denoting that part of him which had not yet been regenerated. Luther also (and increasingly as his life progressed) limited the reference to spiritual temptation. He did not, however, rule out external persecution; but, in Lightfoot's words 'he inclined more and more to the view that spiritual trials were intended, faint-heartedness in Paul's ministerial duties, temptations to despair or doubt, blasphemous suggestions of the devil'.[1]

As there is nothing which tends to elate a Christian evangelist so much as the enjoyment of spiritual experiences, and as there is nothing so calculated to deflate the spiritual pride which may follow them as the opposition he encounters while preaching the Word, it is not unlikely that Chrysostom's interpretation is nearer the truth than any other. It is interesting to notice that it has the support of the Roman Catholic scholar and translator, R. A. Knox, who writes: 'There is one humiliation that permanently irritates St. Paul. Not a physical illness, as the modern Protestants think; the "infirmities" are those of the mind, all through this passage. Nor even temptations against purity, as most Catholic commentators assume, for pulpit purposes; more likely persecutions by the Jews, continually shaming him before the Gentile world (so Augustine, Chrysostom, and the Greek fathers generally).'[2] Knox's own

[1] *The Epistle to the Galatians*, p. 189.
[2] R. A. Knox, *The Epistle and Gospels*, p. 79.

translation of Vulg. is 'a sting to distress my outward nature'; and in a footnote he maintains that the above exegesis is favoured by the reference in Nu. xxxiii. 55. There Moses is bidden to give this warning to the children of Israel when they are about to enter Canaan: 'If ye will not drive out the inhabitants of the land from before you; then shall those which ye let remain of them be as pricks in your eyes, and as thorns in your sides, and they shall vex you in the land wherein ye dwell' (RV).

It may also be argued that this view gives the best explanation of the *messenger of Satan*. For, while Satan is portrayed in Jb. ii. 5 as the agent of physical disease, and the bent woman in Lk. xiii. 16 is described as one 'whom Satan hath bound', he is also presented as the adversary who interferes with the spread of the gospel. Thus in Acts xiii. 10, Elymas the sorcerer who endeavoured 'to turn aside the proconsul from the faith' is addressed by Paul as 'thou son of the devil'; and in 1 Thes. ii. 18, Satan is said to have prevented Paul more than once from paying a much-desired visit to the Thessalonians. Wherever Paul went, he met with opposition both to himself and to his gospel, most frequently from those who were his 'kinsmen according to the flesh' (Rom. ix. 3). This satanic resistance was, in the providence of God, the means by which he was prevented from being 'exalted overmuch'.

The present tense of the verb *to buffet me* seems to imply that the trouble was permanent. And the word itself, *kolaphizō*, means literally 'to strike a blow with the fist', and so 'to maltreat', especially in such a manner that shame and indignation are felt by the sufferer. Paul was humiliated by the 'thorn in the flesh', just as Jesus was humiliated by His buffeting at the hands of the chief priests (Mt. xxvi. 67). The opposition that his presence and his preaching aroused was something Paul found it difficult to understand, especially in the light of the abundance of his revelations. Probably the hardest and most humiliating task of an evangelist, until, like his Master, he has learned obedience through the things he suffers, is to go on faithfully preaching the gospel whether men will hear or whether they will forbear.

8, 9. Jesus prayed three times that the humiliation and the suffering which He had been called upon to endure as the Sin-bearer of mankind might pass from Him. So Paul prayed *thrice* to his risen Master, that the 'thorn in the flesh' *might depart* from him. His prayer was not answered in the way he had at first wished; nevertheless, the answer he received remained with him as the most powerful inspiration in his life. In the original, *he said* is in the perfect tense; and, though the perfect is often used for the aorist, it may here have been used deliberately. For, as Hodge well comments, 'The answer was not simply something past, but something which continued in its consoling power. It was ever sounding in the apostle's ears, and not in his ears only, but in those of all his suffering people from that day to this. . . . It should be engraven on the palm of every believer's hand.'

My grace is sufficient for thee. Paul is here told that whenever he is humiliated by the 'buffeting' he receives, he is to remember that he is the unworthy object of God's unceasing favour; that it was solely by God's unmerited grace that he, the one-time persecutor of God's Church, was called to be an apostle of Jesus Christ; and that God never withdraws His favour from His elect until they have accomplished the work He has assigned them. As *the Lord* in verse 8 refers primarily to Christ, the divine grace is Christ's grace; for it is from His cross, through the merits of His atoning death, that grace proceeds. It is all-sufficient; for, so far from humiliating circumstances being an obstacle to its manifestation, they alone satisfy the condition under which it is most fully experienced and acknowledged; for, as Calvin comments, 'it is not perfected unless it openly shines forth, so as to receive its due praise'. Calvin's further comment is also worthy of quotation: 'The valleys are watered with rain to make them fruitful, while in the meantime the summits of the lofty mountains remain dry. Let that man therefore become a valley who desires to receive the heavenly rain of God's spiritual grace.'

Paul, it is clear, had learned to give due praise for this wonderful paradox of the divine dispensation. *Most gladly therefore,* he says, *will I rather glory in my infirmities*. This is not the cry of a fanatic rejoicing in pain. Paul's glorying rests on the assurance that only in this low estate will he be protected by the over-shadowing *power of Christ*. The expression *may rest upon me* means literally, 'may pitch his tent upon me', i.e. as Hodge comments, 'may dwell in me as in a tent, as the shechinah dwelt of old in the tabernacle' (see Ex. xl. 34).

10. The glorying by the apostle in his infirmities is the out-come of his inward feelings about them. So conscious is he of the all-sufficient grace of Christ, that he takes pleasure in any affliction he is called upon to endure *for Christ's sake*. These last all-important words qualify all the five preceding nouns. Only a morbid fanatic can take pleasure in the sufferings he inflicts upon himself; only an insensitive fool can take pleasure in the sufferings that are the consequences of his folly; and only a convinced Christian can take pleasure in sufferings endured *for Christ's sake*, for he alone has been initiated into the divine secret, that it is only when he is *weak*, having thrown himself unreservedly in penitence and humility upon the never-failing mercies of God, that he is *strong*, with a strength not his own, but belonging to the 'Lord of all power and might'.

i. Paul's behaviour at Corinth on previous visits (xii. 11-13)

11. The words *in glorying* are omitted in the oldest MSS, and the sentence is more vigorous without them. So RSV, 'I have been a fool! You forced me to it'. However much his self-vindication might be justified, Paul cannot but feel that all self-praise is folly, and that in his own case there should have been no need for it. The Corinthians were to blame in so far as they had failed to defend their apostle against his detractors. It was not as though there were not strong grounds on which they could have made a defence. On the contrary, his activities at Corinth were proof that he was *in nothing . . . behind the very chiefest apostles*. This last expression is the same as that used in xi. 5, and it should be regarded here, as there, as ironical (RSV 'these superlative apostles'), and not, as the older commentators tended to interpret it, as a reference to the original apostles. Paul's opponents very probably regarded him as *nothing*, a mere nonentity of an apostle. He is ready to admit this—but only in the sense that everything that makes him worthy of being an apostle has been received by him as a divine gift. By the grace of God he was what he was.

12. As proof that he was not inferior to these other self-styled apostles Paul mentions *the signs of an apostle* that had been *wrought* (i.e. by God through His servant) among them. In this opening expression *signs* is a comprehensive term; it includes the supernatural qualities with which God endowed an apostle, as well as the supernatural activities in which those qualities found expression. In the second reference to *signs*, the meaning is limited by the context to miraculous actions. The oldest MSS omit *in* before this second mention of *signs*; and the meaning is 'by' or 'with' *signs, and wonders, and mighty deeds*. *Patience* is not itself a 'sign', as Calvin imagined. What Paul is saying is that these signs were wrought under conditions of outward trial and tribulation which called for much *patience* (better, 'steadfastness') on his part. Paul limits himself to these eternal manifestations of God's power, because the false apostles laid great emphasis upon the working of miracles as evidence for true apostleship.

Signs, and wonders, and mighty deeds are not three different kinds of miracles, but *all* miracles viewed from three separate angles. In Calvin's words: 'Paul calls them *signs*, because they are not empty shows, but are appointed for the instruction of mankind; *wonders*, because they ought, by their novelty, to arouse men and strike them with astonishment; and *mighty deeds*, because they are more signal tokens of divine power than what we behold in the ordinary course of nature.' In other words, miracles are not meaningless exhibitions of force. They invariably have a didactic purpose. That this was recognized by Jesus when He performed His miracles is clear from such a passage as Mk. ii. 10: 'But that ye may know that the Son of man hath power on earth to forgive sins (he saith to the sick of the palsy), I say unto thee, Arise, and take up thy bed.' After the resurrection, miracles were performed by the apostles to corroborate the truth of the doctrine they preached (see Acts v. 12, xiv. 3; Heb. ii. 4).

13. In verse 11 Paul asserted that in nothing was he inferior to his opponents. This carried with it the implication that the church at Corinth had been well and properly founded. It was an apostolic church, in no way *inferior to other churches*. He now recalls that his refusal to live at the expense of his converts at Corinth, though he accepted help from other churches, might have been misconstrued as something derogatory to the status of the church of God at Corinth. In fact, the Corinthians had benefited by being made an exception in this matter. Paul now, with irony, treats this gain of the Corinthians as if it was an injury inflicted upon them by himself, and asks them to forgive him! So RSV, in company with many modern commentators following Calvin. Others, however, find no irony in the passage. Paul, they feel, is sincerely asking the Corinthians to forgive him, because he is aware that he has given them the impression that he doubted their willingness to assist him by accepting help from other churches and refusing to accept it from them. But this interpretation would seem to be less probable than the other, particularly if the passage is viewed in the light of xi. 7–11.

j. Paul's behaviour on his proposed visit (xii. 14–21)

14. Paul's *third* visit to Corinth is imminent; and, however much his principle of refusing to accept contributions from the Corinthians may have been misunderstood, he does not propose to abandon it on the next occasion—and for two very good reasons. First, he does not want their possessions; he wants themselves. Calvin gives the following excellent paraphrase of the apostle's words: 'I am in quest of a larger hire than you think of. I am not contented with your wealth, but I seek to have you wholly, that I may present a sacrifice to the

Lord of the fruits of my ministry.' It was not that the acceptance of payment from them would of itself render him a hire-
ling and no true shepherd; but that his refusal to accept it
would make it abundantly clear that the faithful shepherd
always has as his primary motive the welfare of his sheep.

Secondly, Paul wishes the Corinthians to have abundant
evidence that he stands to them spiritually *in loco parentis*. As
Hodge well remarks, Paul is saying, in effect, 'You must allow
me a parent's privilege'. Who ever heard of children starting a
banking account for the benefit of their parents! But how right
and proper that parents should lay up for their children,
particularly in days when there was no 'welfare state'.

15. In response to the promptings of his paternal heart
Paul *will very gladly spend* his time, his money, and his strength
in the service of the Corinthians; and in so doing *be spent* out
himself. The price to be paid might well be impoverished
health and premature old age; but such a price was not too
great in so high an endeavour.

The reading of the later MSS underlying AV suggests that the
more the apostle might love the Corinthians, the less love
would he receive in return. The literal translation of this text is
'even if by loving you the more I should be loved the less'.
The older MSS, however, omit 'even' and instead of 'loving' read
'I love'. If this text is adopted, the last half of the verse does
not depend on the first, as in AV, but is a separate conditional
sentence, the apodosis of which is in the form of a question.
So RV, 'If I love you more abundantly, am I loved the less?'
Menzies rightly accepts this much better attested reading, but
regards it as 'harsher' than the other. Written words can never
fully convey the tone in which they would be spoken; but is it
not possible to read this as a question asked with great tenderness, and conveying a most moving appeal?

16. By *be it so* Paul implies that, even if he has successfully
cleared himself of the charge of having sinister motives for
refusing to receive monetary payment from the Corinthians,
there is an even more damaging insinuation being made

about him, about which he must disillusion them. It is being said that *being crafty* he has in fact *caught* the Corinthians *with guile*. He has obtained the money, which he would not accept from them in person, by underhand methods. He has purloined for his own use contributions obtained from them by his agents!

17, 18. There was only one person beside Paul who had been actively concerned with raising money at Corinth, and that was Titus, who had begun the collection in the previous year (see viii. 6). But there was also an unnamed brother, known to the Corinthians, who had often rendered trustworthy service to the apostle in matters of this kind (see viii. 22). Paul has indicated in chapter viii that he is sending these two representatives back to Corinth to complete the work done by Titus. It is probable that in these verses the reference is to this same mission. In verse 17, Paul challenges the Corinthians to recall anything said or done by these men in the past which could have reasonably given the impression that Paul was using them as a means whereby he could *make a gain of* (RV 'take advantage of') them.

In verse 18, the verbs *desired* and *sent*, the former in the perfect tense in the original and the latter in the aorist, are translated with a reference to the past in AV, RV, and RSV. By this rendering the allusion must be, either to the original visit of Titus a year ago, or to the occasion when he was the bearer of the painful letter. But the verbs could equally well be treated as 'epistolary' in character, and translated by the English present, as in Menzies' translation 'I am asking Titus and I am sending the brother with him'. These men have not arrived at Corinth at the time when 2 Corinthians is being written, but they will have done so by the time the Corinthians receive it.

This grammatical point has an important, if indirect, bearing upon the unity of the Epistle. As Menzies says, with much justification: 'This passage shows decisively that chapter xii was not written before chapter viii. In both chapters we hear of the same persons as going from Paul to Corinth about money matters; Titus and the brother. The same verbs are used in both passages to describe their mission; Paul "is asking" Titus to go, and "is sending" the brother with him. In chapter viii, however, the financial envoys are presented to the Corinthians . . . and this passage in which they are introduced is evidently earlier than the passage in chapter xii where they are simply mentioned and it is taken for granted that the Corinthians know about them and their errand.'

As the Corinthians are best acquainted with Titus, Paul bids them recall his previous visits, in a series of questions, the first of which expects the answer 'No', and the second and third the answer 'Yes'. In the second question AV assumes that *in the same spirit* means 'with the same spirit of goodwill'. As the second and third questions are parallel, this translation seems preferable to RV, 'by the same Spirit', which assumes a reference to the truth that Paul and Titus were inspired and guided by the Holy Spirit. *In the same steps* means that the actions of both men accorded with their inward spirit of goodwill.

19. The reading of the older MSS *palai* (RV 'all this time', RSV 'all along') gives a better sense than the reading *palin*, *again*. Paul, either in the form of a statement (RV), or a question (RSV), reveals his awareness that all the time the Corinthians have been listening to his somewhat protracted explanation about his financial relationship with them they may have been feeling that he is making excuses for himself in front of them his judges. He disillusions them on this point. They are not his judges (cf. 1 Cor. iv. 3); but they *are* his *dearly beloved*. His statements, even on comparatively unimportant matters, such as the one under discussion, are made with the consciousness that he is standing in the presence of the all-seeing God, and that he is a man living in union with Christ. Everything is said without any desire unduly to impress them, but entirely for their 'upbuilding' (RSV) as members of the body of Christ.

20. This 'upbuilding' involves the elimination of every-thing that prevents the healthy growth of Christian fellow-ship. Much of this work of elimination still remains to be done at Corinth, for there is a minority of Christians in the city, who are still carnally-minded and undisciplined in the school of Christ. Paul fears that 'the jealous factious spirit by which all Greek public life was haunted, and against which his first warnings to Corinth had been directed' (Menzies) may still be spoiling their common life, and may take away much of the happiness of the forthcoming visit both for himself and them. He therefore analyses the ingredients of this obnoxious poison. For *debates* and *envyings* RV, translating the older read-ing which has the same nouns in the singular, has 'strife' and 'jealousy'. *Wraths* renders *thumoi*, which means 'fits of temper'. *Strifes* represent *eritheiai*, a word akin to *ereis*, the first word in the list, but stressing the idea of partisanship; it might be accurately rendered 'party-intrigues'. By *backbitings, katalaliai,* are probably meant slanders spoken behind people's backs; and by *whisperings, psithurismoi,* defamations in the forms of innuendos. *Swellings, phusiōseis,* refer to bombastic manifesta-tions of pride; and *tumults, akatastasiai,* are the disorders that must inevitably afflict a body politic when it is riddled with faction and intrigue.

21. Paul speaks again of his apprehensiveness about his forthcoming visit. Instead of experiencing legitimate pride in the progress of his converts, he may be humbled by God *among* (RV, better, 'before') them, as he sees them still carnal and not yet controlled by the Holy Spirit. Instead of rejoicing over them in the Lord, he may have to mourn their failure to abandon pagan ways. Some of them, he fears, may be still unrepentant of the immorality which they have continued to practise even after their conversion.

The three words here used to depict this immorality are not synonyms. The first, *uncleanness, akatharsia,* is a general term for 'the impurity of lustful, luxurious and profligate living'.[1] The

---

[1] So Grimm and Thayer, *Greek-English Lexicon of the New Testament.*

second word, *fornication*, *porneia*, is limited to promiscuous sexual intercourse, especially prostitution and fornication; while the third, *lasciviousness*, *aselgeia*, describes misconduct committed with a wilful defiance of public decency.

k. Paul's determination to restore discipline at Corinth (xiii. 1–10)

1. Paul's greatest desire in this letter is that all shall be well on his forthcoming third visit to Corinth; but the peace that he longs for is not a peace at any price. So far from overlooking the charges which some of his detractors may still be making against him, he will investigate them on his arrival with judicial thoroughness. The truth or falsehood of each indictment will be established by him in accordance with the law of evidence laid down in Dt. xix. 15, a law which Jesus commanded His disciples to follow and with which He Himself complied (see Mt. xviii. 16; Jn. viii. 17).

2. By three legitimate changes a more intelligible rendering of this verse can be given than that found in AV. (a) The words *I write* are absent from the oldest authorities for the text and should be omitted. (b) The participle *parōn*, rendered conditionally *as if I were present*, should be taken in a temporal sense as in RV 'as when I was present'. (c) The words *being absent now* should be construed with the verb *foretell*. RV has made these changes, but by slavishly following the order of the Greek words has produced a clumsy English sentence. RSV rightly redrafts the sentence, 'I warned those who sinned before and all the others, and I warn them now while absent, as I did when present on my second visit. . . .' Paul repeats the warning given on the painful visit for the benefit not only of the offenders at Corinth already known to him, but of all others who may need it.

The expression *if I come again* does not imply that, humanly speaking, there is any doubt about it. The Greek conditional particle *ean* often has the meaning 'when' as in Jn. xvi. 7 and 1 Jn. iii. 2. We cannot then assume with Rendall that 'the resolution is not yet unutterably fixed', and use the expression as he does as additional support for the theory that chapter xiii does not belong to the final letter written by Paul to Corinth. Still less justifiable is Rendall's interpretation of *if I come again* as 'If I am forced to come again'.

The stern words *I will not spare* remind us, as Hodge comments, that 'the apostolic churches were not independent democratic communities, vested with supreme authority over their own members. Paul could cast out of them whom he would'.

3. The apostle will not hesitate to exercise this spiritual authority, if necessary, when he arrives at Corinth, not because he desires to magnify his own importance, but because, in challenging the validity of his apostleship, his detractors are in effect denying that he is a *bona fide* messenger of Christ. They wanted, he says, *a proof of Christ speaking in me*. Paul had failed to give them evidence which they would have regarded as unmistakable that he really possessed the spiritual authority of an apostle of Christ. Paul now asserts that he is ready to give them the proof they desire. When he restores order at Corinth by not hesitating to use drastic measures, it will become evident that Christ is speaking in him, Christ *which to you-ward is not weak, but is mighty in you*. Some commentators suppose that in these words Paul is reminding the Corinthians of the manifestation of Christ's power in their conversion and generally in their life as Christians; but in the light of the context the words would seem to have a more specific and limited reference.

4. The Christ with whom the Corinthians, and all Christians, have to deal is a living Christ who possesses all authority (see Mt. xxviii. 18). It is true, Paul admits, that there was a time when weakness rather than strength seemed His most obvious characteristic. He assumed human nature with all its weakness so that He might be capable of submitting to the most ignominious of deaths. As He hung on the cross He seemed to be completely at the mercy of sinners. But *though he was crucified* *through* (i.e. under the conditions of) *weakness, yet he liveth by the power of God*. As Paul says in Rom. vi. 10 (rsv), 'The death he died he died to sin, once for all, but the life he lives he lives to God'. 'The cross', as Denney so pertinently comments, 'does not exhaust Christ's relation to sin. He passes from the cross to the throne, and when He comes again it is as Judge.'

Though the way trodden by Christ for man's salvation was unique, nevertheless those who are *in him* can be said to have some share in His *weakness*, when they show forbearance and submission in the face of the opposition of sinners. Paul admits that on his last visit to Corinth his failure to vindicate his authority could be described as 'weakness' in this sense. Like his Master on Calvary he seemed for the moment to have been an impotent victim. But just as Christ was raised from the dead, so he, sharing as he does in Christ's risen life, will himself reflect the greatness of His power should he be called upon to pass sentence at Corinth upon the disobedient.

There is no direct reference to the future life of believers in the words *we shall live with him*. The omission however of the words *toward you* (rsv 'in dealing with you') in B may well be due to the desire of some early scribe to give the passage this wider reference.

5, 6. Paul's defamers at Corinth have been in effect submitting him to an examination, calling upon him to show proof of his spiritual authority; and some of the Corinthians have been lending them too ready an ear. The emphatic position in the Greek of *yourselves* and *your own selves* shows that Paul is here turning the tables upon them. It is they, not he, who should submit to examination. Let them look into their own souls, and they will see that their attitude in this matter is not in keeping with the faith they profess. The apostle seems to be reminding them that after all they *are* Christians, for in the appeal, *know ye not your own selves, how that Jesus Christ is in you, except ye be reprobates?*, he is in effect dismissing the idea that they will in fact fail to stand the test, just as in verse 6 he expresses the certain hope that from the evidence that he is ready to give them, should it be needed, they will be compelled to see that he is no reprobate. If each Corinthian Christian puts himself to the test he will conclude, Paul is convinced, that Jesus Christ is in him; that he is, in Menzies' words, 'approved before God, and will not have to dread the apostle's severity'.

7. Paul does not, however, wish to show this severity. Hence his prayer that the behaviour of the Corinthians may be such that he will not have to give them this particular evidence of Christ speaking in him, which he is prepared to give. It is true, in that happy eventuality, that Paul will be deprived of the opportunity of vindicating himself by giving what would be considered clear evidence that he is indeed an approved apostle of Christ. But what would it matter if he and his companions had to pass *as reprobates*, so long as the behaviour of his converts was *honest*.

8. The connection between this and the previous verse, indicated by *For*, is not easy to determine. The basic assumption would, however, seem to be that the main aim of the preaching of the gospel is that men should do what is well-pleasing and acceptable to God. If that result should be achieved only by the apostle appearing in the sight of men as reprobate, i.e. as a man whose claims have not been vindicated with unmistakable clearness to others, then he is content that it should be so. By *the truth* is meant 'the gospel'. To proclaim the gospel under all circumstances and by every means in his power, and to refrain from everything that might hinder its advance, is the master aim of the apostle's life. Denney draws attention to the supreme importance for every Christian minister of the great simplifying principle enunciated in this verse. 'It is by-ends that explain nine-tenths of spiritual inefficiency; singleness of mind like this would save us our perplexities and our failures.'

9. But Paul is not only *content* to be *as reprobate*, if the progress of the gospel should have this as its accompaniment; he is even *glad* to be so. He is *glad* that he should be *weak*, bereft of the opportunity to exercise his legitimate power to punish and exert his strength, if such 'weakness' should be due to the 'strength', i.e. the moral goodness, of his converts. That they should be *strong* in this sense, and that they should be continually perfecting their weaknesses is the supreme object of his prayer. The same Greek word rightly translated as *pray* in verse 7 is somewhat misleadingly rendered *wish* in this verse. *Perfection* is better translated 'perfecting' (RV) or 'improvement' (RSV), as the Greek word *katartismon* suggests the idea of repairing what is broken and restoring what is lost rather than of bringing what is already good to perfection.

10. The severe note sounded by Paul in the last chapters of this Epistle is due to the apostle's intense concern that his third visit to the Corinthians should be no repetition of the second. He prefers to write what is painful rather than to have to say it in person. In any case, whether they are written now or spoken then, certain things must be made clear to them because they are inherent in the proper exercise of his apostolic authority. That authority was bestowed upon him by Christ Himself, who is concerned that it should be used to further the ends of His kingdom. Its ultimate purpose is not destructive but constructive (see x. 8); and, even when he is called upon to take what appear to be destructive measures, the end in view is always the *edification* of God's people. The apostle is hopeful that the truth set forth in this section of the letter will have done its work by the time he arrives at Corinth, and that he will then have no need to *use sharpness* either by punishing or excommunicating.

VIII. CONCLUSION (xiii. 11–14)

11. As Paul brings his correspondence with the Corinthians to a close, he makes a fourfold appeal to them. First, he bids them, not so much to *be perfect*, but rather to make good their deficiencies (RSV 'mend your ways'), for the verb *katartizesthe* is cognate with the noun used in verse 9. Secondly, he would have them *be of good comfort*, remembering that God, as he had reminded them in i. 3, is 'the God of all comfort'. It is possible, however, that the word *parakaleisthe* has here its other meaning 'be exhorted' (so RSV 'heed my appeal'). Thirdly, he urges them to foster a common mutual outlook by putting first things first as Paul made it his aim to do (see note on verse 8). Fourthly, he in effect reminds them that the peace of Christian fellowship is marred by sectional enthusiasm and exaggerated personal loyalties. If these four injunctions are obeyed, then the church at Corinth will indeed be the Church of God, whose greatest characteristic is love and 'from whom alone all thoughts of truth and peace proceed'.

12, 13. The *holy kiss*, with which they were accustomed to greet one another when they met for worship, must be no meaningless formality, but the outward and visible sign of that mutual charity born of a common response to the love of their Lord for them, which should characterize all Christian people. Prompted by that charity, the Christians in Paul's company at the time he is writing send their greetings to the brethren in Corinth, though for the most part they are personally unknown to them.

14. In this wonderful closing verse, among the most frequently quoted words in the Pauline Epistles, the apostle adds his customary final prayer that his readers may live in the atmosphere of that saving *grace*, whose *fons et origo* is the redemptive death of the *Lord Jesus Christ*. But he does more than this. Here, and nowhere else in his extant letters, he prays further that they may experience *the love of God*, of which Christ's sacrifice on Calvary was the outstanding revelation, and also that fellowship which the Holy Spirit creates among all who have stood beneath the cross and accepted Christ as their personal Saviour. As the first of the three genitives in this verse must be subjective, it is probable that the other two should be construed in the same way. It is not the Christian's love for God, nor his communion with the Holy Spirit that is here the dominant thought, but rather the love displayed by God and the fellowship achieved by the Holy Spirit.

This verse provides part of the New Testament data for the doctrine of the Holy Trinity; and the unusual order in which the three Persons are mentioned reminds us that in the thought of the early Church about the nature of God the redemption wrought by Christ had a primary place. There can be no adequate understanding of God's love apart from the cross; and the only lasting fellowship between men is the fellowship of sinners redeemed by the blood of Jesus.